T0209575

Narrow

A Guide for Women to a Successful Marriage and Thriving Family

KATIE HEDGES

WESTBOW
PRESS®
A DIVISION OF THOMAS NELSON
& ZONDERVAN

NASB: "Scripture taken from the NEW AMERICAN STANDARD BIBLE®, Copyright © 1960,1962,1963,1968,1971,1972,1973,1975,1977,1995 by The Lockman Foundation. Used by permission. www.Lockman.org"

NIV: THE HOLY BIBLE, NEW INTERNATIONAL VERSION®, NIV® Copyright © 1973, 1978, 1984, 2011 by Biblica, Inc.® Used by permission. All rights reserved worldwide.

Front and back cover by Janis Day

WestBow Press books may be ordered through booksellers or by contacting:

WestBow Press
A Division of Thomas Nelson & Zondervan
1663 Liberty Drive
Bloomington, IN 47403
www.westbowpress.com
1 (866) 928-1240

ISBN: 978-1-9736-5276-2 (sc)
ISBN: 978-1-9736-5277-9 (hc)
ISBN: 978-1-9736-5275-5 (e)

Library of Congress Control Number: 2019901174

Print information available on the last page.

WestBow Press rev. date: 02/07/2019

CONTENTS

INTRODUCTION

I t's a balancing act, I've found. Life, that is.
It's learning how to stay on the beam - by falling off of it... and landing flat on your face.

A lot.

This is the most appropriate place to introduce myself, for two reasons. One, because, well, it's the Introduction, and that's just what I'm supposed to do. And two, because I'm a pro - not at the balance beam... but at falling flat on my face.

A lot.

So, hey... I'm Katie. And this is my Introduction, which, by the way, is really more like its own chapter as opposed to a simple preface, but hey, this is my book after all, and I'm not one to follow a mold anyway!

So a little about me....

When I began writing this book, I was a know-it-all in my twenties. I had all the answers to having a successful marriage and thriving family. After all, I'd been married for a few years, and had a couple kids by then. I'd perfected the marriage and family balance beam, you see. Ha.

So, having mastered life, and with the best of intentions, I set out on this journey of authoring with the sincere desire to help others achieve what I had. Thankfully, though, the Lord chose to give me a few good years of humbling before I published all my knowledge!

Fast forward those few more years, a couple more kids, and a LOT of said humbling from the Lord (and consequently a LOT of editing my manuscript), and my dream of authoring this book has finally come to fruition, at the (still very young) age of thirty-two.

But, I'm no longer a know-it-all. In fact, I know less now than I did even five years ago - a trend I imagine will continue as I age. Funny how that works.

That said, though, my desire to help others have a successful marriage and family is still there, and the narrow beam we all have to walk in order to achieve that success is still the same. I've just learned how to balance on it a little better now. And I've learned the key to that balancing act is grace. And for the record, I'm still walking the beam... and still falling flat on my face more than I care to admit. But I'm happy to share what I've learned thus far.

As I write this, I'm enjoying my tenth year of being married to my wonderful husband; I'm absolutely loving my job as a stay-at-home mama, to now four beautiful gifts from God; I'm in my seventh year of homeschooling, and I guess now I'm an author too!

Most importantly, though, I am an unashamed Christian; and while I've learned the beauty of grace, I'm still extremely (socially) conservative, very opinionated, politically incorrect, and considered by many (ok, most) absolutely crazy. But guess what? My family is happy. Content. Joyful. And we love Jesus. Aka, successful.

My goal with this book is not to present you with a know-it-all, cookie cutter mold created for you by me, designed for you to squeeze your family into, but rather it is to present the basic truths of God's design for your marriage and family, and give you a glimpse into our lives - a look at our walk on the balance beam; all to show you that narrow living, at the direction of the Holy Spirit, will always achieve success. It will always need grace, but it will always achieve the success of contentment. It *deeply* saddens me to see so many people living in an unsuccessful marriage with a mediocre family life, and I want to do what I can to help even just one family.

Before you ask, the answer is no. No, I don't have all the answers. No, I don't know exactly what your situation is. No, I can't promise that, should you be searching for that successful marriage and family, even if you mimicked my every conviction, God would restore your failing marriage or bring your prodigal child home. We live in a fallen world, where bad things just happen; sometimes for no specific reason, and sometimes, because we must reap the consequences of the sins of our past, and even those of generations before us. But there is hope, hence I've kept writing. I see so many people struggling when they just don't have to. And while God, in His sovereignty, may not restore or mend every relationship out there, it's certainly worth the effort on the good chance that He might. God is a God of restoration, of hope, of peace! And He loves us, and wants us to live in unity together by His Word.

That happens because we are intentional in the way we live. And while grace abounds, the way is narrow.

Throughout these pages are woven Biblical truth, historical statistics, helpful how-to's, and many of my own personal convictions, all in hopes to guide you to that place of success (...*success*, not perfection).

I will also preface the pages to follow with a few points:

First -

It's important to understand the difference between personal convictions and Biblical commands.

Like it or not, *some* things are black and white, non-negotiable - Biblical *commands*, for ALL Christians, everywhere.

God said, in His Word, to do (or not to do) certain things, and so, as Christians, we do (or don't) out of our genuine desire to please Him. That's not to say He doesn't show us grace if (and when) we mess up, but it IS to say that we are to strive NOT to mess up in basic Biblical commands (think: the Ten Commandments, for example).

Personal convictions from God, though, are just that - personal. These personal understandings and callings are given to us in our unique circumstances, according to God's desire, so that our obedience may bring about His glory. Of course, certain convictions of *mine* may not be the same as yours, and that's ok - that doesn't make me any better (or worse) than you; however, it's my opinion that if people were truly living sold out for Jesus, we would find that many of us would be convicted in many of the same ways.

My convictions are simply included in these pages to show you what *we* are committed to doing for *our* family and why. They're not included to judge you and your family, or condemn you for living differently. Perhaps, though the Holy Spirit will use them to just get you thinking. Why do you do the things that you do? Is God calling you to something more?

While personal convictions differ from one person to the next, it's important to remember that true convictions from the Holy Spirit will *always* have Scriptural backing. True Godly convictions will *never* go against God's Word.

Furthermore, because they are divinely inspired, as are the commands given to us in the Bible, convictions by the Holy Spirit should be obeyed just the same, for the duration of the season that God chooses.

So, read this book with the mindset that yes, the things I share with you are *my* convictions. They may not ALL be for you (or perhaps they may not all even be possible for you in the unique situation in which God has placed you); however, they have aided in providing *me* with a successful marriage and a thriving family, so perhaps they (or some version of them) can provide *you* with the same thing.

Second -

I've said it a few times already, but I'm going to say it again. The success that I enjoy doesn't mean that I know it all, or that I have all the answers. Yes, I will outline some general guidelines that can lead to your success, but I'll leave the specifics up to you. Just keep in mind that these general guidelines are not just great ideas that I decided to try which happened to work for me. These are steps to take that are Biblically backed, and statistically proven to work.

As you will see, it was only after I decided to surrender all of *my* 'great ideas' of success that I actually achieved it. I'm following Someone else's plan, and just like He promised, it's working! All I've done is recorded how I followed (and continue to follow!) it, in order to share that success with you. So even if you're not a Christian, or maybe not a 'churchy person' (as one of my friends once put it), you might be surprised at God's willingness to restore your family's brokenness if you choose to truly put Him first. It's worth a shot, anyway, right?

I just want to share the ways that He's led me to this place of success with as many women as possible, and I'm so excited to do that with this book.

I'll warn you though.
Should you choose to follow Him, regardless of how He may uniquely call you, it will not be easy.
Furthermore, reading this book will likely shake your current view on a woman's role, thanks to the Feminist Movement.
Some of what I've written might even make you angry.
Results will take time.

But obeying the commands, and following the calls and convictions of God are ALWAYS worth it, and He will ALWAYS provide.

So no matter if you're fighting for your marriage or family solo, or if you have willing participants to ensure success, read these pages with an open mind and the willingness to follow as God leads you - and give it your all. You're willingness and efforts may very likely be the thing to save your marriage or your family. I have seen it time and time again. Your marriage and family are worth fighting for - to the death.

I want you to see the goal you have in front of you. I want you to see the finish line. And I want you to fight like you've never fought for anything before to achieve that.
And I'm gonna be right there on the sidelines cheering you on, throughout the pages of this book.

It is my prayer that each of you who reads this book will first find salvation in Jesus Christ, and secondly, enjoy a successful marriage and a thriving family, just like I do every day!

PART 1

"How-to", "What-to-do", & "You've got to be kidding"!

Warning: Prepare for a little discomfort. ….Or a lot.
Commit to yourself *now* to read this book from start to finish, regardless of how crazy you begin to think I am. You don't want to miss the solutions that God may lead you to because you let your emotions get in the way. Also, remember, as you read – I, too, once had to set my emotions aside and face these tough answers myself, prior to finding that sweet spot of success!

ONE

The Beginning

The beginning is always the best place to start, right? Right, so let's start there - *before* we analyze our own lives or current situations and *before* we make a checklist of what we want to change. Let's forget all that right now and start at the beginning.

Of time.

The beginning of man, or in our specific case, woman, which we find in Genesis 2:15-22:

15 Then the LORD God took the man and put him into the garden of Eden to cultivate it and keep it. 16 The LORD God commanded the man, saying, "From any tree of the garden you may eat freely; 17 but from the tree of the knowledge of good and evil you shall not eat, for in the day that you eat from it you will surely die." 18 Then the LORD God said, "It is not good for the man to be alone; I will make him a helper suitable for him." 19 Out of the ground the LORD God formed every beast of the field and every bird of the sky, and brought them to the man to see what he would call them; and whatever the man called a living creature, that was its name. 20 The man gave names to all the cattle, and to the birds of the sky, and to every beast of the field, but for Adam there was not found a helper suitable for him. **²¹** *So the LORD God caused a deep sleep to fall upon the man, and he slept; then He took one of his ribs and closed up the flesh at that place.* **²²** *The LORD God fashioned into a woman the rib which He had taken from the man, and brought her to the man."*

Now most of us have probably at least heard part of that story before (it's ok if you haven't though!); but let's move a step past *hearing* and actually *dissect* it, because it's FULL of things we need to recognize and embrace in order to understand just how God wants us to carry out the necessary applications to success.

First, let's go back and read verse 22, *"The LORD God fashioned into a woman the rib which He had taken from the man, and brought her to the man."*

OK, there are two very important things to take from this verse:

#1 - We were fashioned by God.

Ladies, we were fashioned, or created, by *God* - the God of the Universe, Who loves us beyond our wildest imagination.
Talk about worth! We've got it!
No matter who we are, what we do, what we've *done*, what we look like... we have worth enough for God to have fashioned *us*. Each of us.
That's big.

#2 - We, as women, were created *second* to man *for the man.*

GULP.

Wait, wait, wait! Don't quit reading!! Don't throw this book in the trash! You want success in your marriage and family, right? I told you I'm not politically correct - you were forewarned! Just trust me and keep reading. Now, take a deep breath and let's read that again.

Woman was created second to man for the man.

Those two little words, 'second' and 'for'. They go against EVERYTHING the Feminist Movement embraces and stands for, and as a result, are seen as wrong.

Oh, the Feminist Movement.

In case you don't know exactly what the Feminist Movement is, when it started, or what it led to, allow me to explain with a very brief history lesson:

The Feminist Movement actually began in the early 1900's, with a relatively harmless enactment of legal rights for women - the right to vote and own property. What started out small though, took off in growth in the 1960's, in what's known as the Second Wave of Feminism, when other legal inequalities caused unrest among *a few women*. The fight for further *legal* equality during that time, in turn, led to *social* unrest, and all of a sudden women everywhere began to follow the rebellious lead of *a few women* to search for their worth in equality to men, instead of embracing their God-given roles and responsibilities. As a result, by the 1970's, many women were claiming victory in gender equality without realizing the devastating defeat it was causing to their marriages and families. By the time the Third Wave of Feminism began in the 1990s, the focus on social inequalities reached an all time high, and has just continued to increase at an alarming rate.

Now with this information, and the devastating reality of the current family unit, it might seem fair to place the blame at the feet of women alone, but men are equally - actually more - responsible.

At the beginning of time, remember, woman was given the role of helper, therefore by default, man was ordained by God as the leader. As further proof, we can look at Genesis chapter 3, which highlights the fall of man. We all know the story: Eve ate the fruit, gave it to Adam, and they got in trouble.

Look with me though, specifically at the woman's curse in verse 16:
"To the woman He said, "I will greatly multiply your pain in childbirth, in pain you will bring forth children; Yet your desire will be for your husband, and he will rule over you."

That last part, *'and he will rule over you.'* reiterates the fact that men are to lead women. This verse even addresses the woman's future desire for the man's role (*your desire will be for your husband*), yet clearly establishes man as the leader.

Through this lens, we see that while women inappropriately challenged their God-given roles and responsibilities during the Feminist Movement, men failed to utilize theirs.

Had men exercised their authority over women by resisting the initial rebellion of those few restless women, the Feminist Movement never would have happened; and more importantly, marriages and families wouldn't have suffered such a devastating defeat.

Man's mistake in the Feminist Movement is actually a striking resemblance to his mistake in the Garden: Woman gave into the temptation of rebellion because man allowed her to. Had Adam stepped up like he was created to, he would have stopped Eve from eating that fruit, and in the same way, had men during the 1900's stepped up and stood against the social unrest among women (specifically during the Second Wave of the Feminist Movement), they would have stopped women from searching for their worth in gender equality. One could also make the argument that had men exercised their leadership appropriately in the first place, women never would have reached a place of unrest.

Regardless of who is ultimately to blame, though, it's crucial for us to understand just how devastating the Feminist Movement has been. It has *completely* distorted the worth of a woman's God-given role as a helper, and thrust women into the false idea of needing to be more. As a result, women everywhere began trying to change their role from *helper* to *leader*, all under the deluded impression that a woman's genetic makeup would allow her to thrive in a leadership position. Everyone seemed to forget, though, that God designed us perfectly, and gave us a genetic make up suited perfectly for achieving *our* role as helper, which can not just be 'recalculated' upon our desire to lead. We are by nature (as a whole) more emotional, more compassionate, and more considerate. That's not by mistake... it's by design! God made us to 'help' the man - physically, emotionally, and spiritually, and gave us a genetic makeup to ensure success in our relationships.

Those qualities and characteristics found in our genetic makeup, though, are *only* successful when used in the right way.

I don't question a woman's ability to effectively lead or take control - our gender has proven, through the Feminist Movement, that we can, in many ways.

We effectively take control in the workplace, and move up the career ladder, often quicker than men. We effectively control our family's finances. We're able to control the number of children we have through means of birth control. We effectively lead companies, cities, states. We even lead and control the conversations we have with others, by refusing to be quiet and demanding things be done our way.

No, I'm in agreement that women are absolutely *able* to effectively take control.

What I'm questioning though is the success our control yields.

Do we really have it - success? ...Where it matters?

In our marriage? In our family?

I'll interject here to say that I recognize that not all women get married and have children, and that is ok. While this book is written to offer success in *marriage and family relationships*, I understand that some of you ladies reading may be single, and are probably wondering where taking control (or not taking it) fits in for you.

Without an 'Adam' to lead you through life, what's a girl to do?

The answer is actually pretty simple - you do it yourself, though I do believe a few factors come into play here. If you're a single gal who is anticipating marriage at some point in your future - be it now, or twenty years from now - I believe that you should take that future commitment into consideration by preparing yourself to eventually yield control to your future husband. You may be on your own now, doing things your way, controlling every aspect of your life, and that's good. But *prior* to marriage, you must be willing to give up that control at the necessary point in the future in order to enjoy a successful relationship.

Perhaps, though, you are a single woman who never intends to marry. Maybe you never cared to marry. Maybe you're a single mom whose husband has died. Maybe you have just signed final divorce papers and a future marriage is the last thing on your mind right now. In these (and other exceptional) cases, your life and your decision making ability is yours alone, so ask God to help you make your decisions with confidence, and take control to protect and preserve your own life and the lives of those with whom you have been entrusted (By the way, each of the above examples I listed were intentional examples that apply to different - and very dear - friends of mine right now at this very moment. I include them to show you that I am acutely aware of the fact that we all lead different lives, and that we all have different circumstances. Yet even still, God can and will use our total surrender to Him, and can bless us far beyond our imagination if we are willing!).

So yea, for all you single ladies… just keep in mind that even though you are single, you're still a woman, and still share the same genetic makeup and curse that all women do, and therefore should still fight against gender equality.
It may not be fair, but we all know that life isn't.
And while you may not have a marriage or family relationship in which to see success - embrace your God-given role as a woman right where you are and you will see success in your own life. Guaranteed!
It is my prayer that this book helps you find that perspective!

As this book *is* geared to marriages and families, however, let's address those areas specifically.
So.. wives, mamas.. do we really have success where it matters? Or do we see success in our jobs, our finances, or our conversations… while our *families* just fall apart.
There are a lot of 'successful' ladies out there - those of us who have risen to the top in a career as maybe a CEO, a highly accredited lawyer, or a Presidential candidate.
On the surface, these women haven't just achieved success, they've exceeded it.
But… how does one measure success?
Sure, these ladies' jobs might be booming, their paychecks might be rolling in, but how are their families doing?

How is *your* family doing?

I challenge you to do a little self evaluation. While you may not like these questions, you may like the results of that self evaluation even less. Those results can change though.
Just stick with me.

TWO

Follow the Leader

If you're anything like me, achieving success starts with needing a little bit of encouragement.

I may not feel good about where I'm at in my life at any given point, but in order for me to take steps to change it, I have to have some positive encouragement.

My husband has learned, through my often emotional state, that his profession of love at the altar was great, but I (for some illogical reason) need constant reminding!

In the same way, most women find that a simple reminder, like an 'I love you' or 'you're worth it' is all that's needed to boost their motivation.

Encouragement.

So... ya want some?

Because I've got the ultimate 'I love you, you're worth it'.

Let's take it back to Genesis 2.

This time, let's focus on verse 15, which says *"Then the LORD God took the man and put him into the garden of Eden to cultivate it and keep it."*

So, at this point, God had created almost everything, so it seemed.

Man, named Adam, was placed in the Garden of Eden and put in charge of all of God's wonderful creations. Things seemed complete... except one thing was missing.

A few verses later, is one of my favorite parts of the Bible: verse 18. Here we see God change the pace a little bit. He's just spent six days creating the world and all it's wonders and 'seeing that they were good', but in Genesis 2:18, after His most precious creation of man in His image, He is just simply not satisfied... in fact, He says just that.

Verse 18 says *"Then the LORD God said, "It is not good for the man to be alone; I will make him a helper suitable for him.".*

Day after day, God saw that it was good - until now.

See the change of pace?

It was only after the creation of *woman* that God's creations were complete.

The God of the Universe hung the stars in the sky, formed the Earth with His hands, spoke life into a man, and *still* saw a reason to create woman. How's that for an 'I love you, you're worth it!'?

I mean, do we as women really need more worth than that?

While it may still bother us to think of women being created *second to* and *for* men, if we adjust our perspective, we trade offense for value.

No, man and woman weren't put in the Garden of Eden at the same time, and no, they weren't given the same roles. But their *roles* didn't determine their worth. The *fact that they were created* did.

All the separate roles did was ensure success.

Oftentimes, a Biblical view on the roles and responsibilities of men and women can at first glance seem unfair and degrading, and many people distort the God-ordained inequality in gender by suggesting that God values women less than men.

That simply isn't true.

Take, for example, a business. Different employees are given different roles and responsibilities to ensure that the business is run successfully; and while some may earn more than others, their roles are *equally valued* to the company's success.

The president of an accounting firm may have closed a huge business deal last week, but the office clerk was the one who properly prepared the conference room he met in, so as to ensure the client was comfortable and confident in the firm. The office clerk was the one who had the hot coffee available, a comfy seat prepared, and the copies made. The office clerk was the one who called both parties to remind them of their scheduled meeting, and the office clerk was the one to gather last minute materials needed.

See, both jobs are different, yes, but both jobs are equally important in ensuring success.

Without that clerk, the president would have had to prepare the conference room himself, make the coffee, remember the pen, set the alarm, make the call, grab the files, make the copies, and a hundred other things not mentioned; cutting into the time he could use to focus on closing that deal. Having someone in place to willingly meet those needs, however, made the entire business run more efficiently, and laid the foundation for success.

So to say that the Biblical view of gender inequality implies that women are less valued by God is twisted. Our roles are different. Our worth is not.

So receive the encouragement that you have worth, you have value! You are loved!

Feeling better?

Quit getting hung up on the fact that I just compared you to an office clerk.

I can hear you now. "How dare she suggest that I'm not capable of being the *president* of the accounting firm! She thinks all I'm good for is making coffee and setting out paper!"

JUST STOP. First of all, if *that* was your thought process, you are missing the point *completely*, and you need to go back and reconsider everything I've said up until this point with an *open mind*.

Secondly, for the record - I used to be an office clerk at an accounting firm! When I first got married, I began working for a prominent accounting firm in town, and worked there for over four years, until my first child was born; and I am here to tell you, being an office clerk is *important*. I had so many responsibilities, and so many different hats to wear - far more than simply making coffee and setting out paper. In fact, I loved

my job, and had God not called me to leave for my family, I would likely still be there today!
So get your big girl pants on, and let's move on.

Are you sure we are over that hurdle?
Ok, I'll ask again, are you feeling better about your worth?
Good!

See, God had a plan in establishing our gender roles, and that plan was success!
But we have to do things His way.
We have to oppose the Feminist Movement and embrace our purpose as a woman: to meet a man's needs. Society has told us that we are not good enough if we aren't running the company. Preparing coffee and making copies doesn't sound like a very exciting or challenging existence (as we've already covered), and it seems degrading, sexist, and pathetic to suggest that we do the more tedious and remedial tasks in life.
Just remember, it's all about perspective. Gaining the right perspective allows you to trade offense for value.

Remember Genesis 2:20: *"but for Adam there was not found a helper suitable for him."*?
Like it or not, we were designed to help - to meet the needs man had.
Because that's what he (Adam) *needed* in order for things to be 'good' in the sight of God.

Did you hear me? That's what he needed - a helper.
Not another *leader*. An assistant.

Have you ever heard the phrase 'too many cooks in the kitchen'? It means there's trouble because too many people are trying to do the same thing! The man didn't *need* someone to do the same things he did, he *needed* someone to prepare the conference room for him!

Do you follow me?
Like it or not ladies, we are that assistant.
Remember, we are by nature (as a whole) more emotional, more compassionate, more considerate - all of which are needed in our task of

helping men (Consider those characteristics! Why do you think *women* give birth and not men!?).

God didn't create a woman because *He* needed a woman. He created a woman because the *man* needed her. Again, look at our worth! We are needed, we are valued! As a *helper*! Why look for equality with men when men *need* us in the very role we're running from?

The Feminist Movement started as a subtle opposition to God's perfect design, but has turned into blatant disrespect. To say that women should strive for gender equality is undermining God's sovereignty in His perfect design of women.

It's no surprise to look at statistics during the Feminist Movement, specifically those of the 1960's, and see drastic changes in families for the worse.

Prior to the Second Wave of Feminism, even popular women's magazines encouraged married women to embrace their expected duties as a *helper* to their husband.

These magazines (and other media) actually encouraged wives to do things such as prepare themselves before their husband arrived home from work by touching up their make-up, or brushing their hair, etc. Wives were encouraged to have the children cleaned up and quiet upon their husband's return home. All noisy appliances were suggested to be shut off, rooms were to be kept tidy, and of course a delicious meal was expected to be prepared and waiting on a set table.

A wife was even suggested to go above and beyond her typical housewife duties. She was to consider the long day her husband likely had at work, and therefore refrain from asking lots of questions, or complaining about petty problems. Things like greeting him at the door with a smile, taking his shoes off for him, offering him a cool drink and a comfortable prepared place to sit were all valuable and very normal suggestions.

And yes, women actually bought these magazines!

Our media is a tad bit different today, huh? We now live in time where a 'good wife' is pictured on our television screen as a woman who juggles a husband, children, home, and a full time career; has an affair with a former lover; and due to her unhappiness, later divorces her husband.

And no one bats an eye; while, to most women today, the way of living from the 1950's (and prior) is so 'outdated' that it's laughable, even insulting.

Keep in mind though, we're on the other side of the Feminist Movement, so we've been ingrained to think that way from society.

But I say, "be not like dumb driven cattle!"

This 'outdated' way of life for an average woman seems very strange to us over fifty years later, but it was prevalent, and was considered important and rewarding. Furthermore, the statistics of that generation show success in the vast majority of marriage and families.

In 1950, only two out of every ten marriages ended in divorce.

That generation may seem silly for their way of having done things, but they hold the most successful stats for marriages and families.

Coincidence? I think not.

Fast forward twenty years to the height of the rise of feminism, and let's compare the decades' lasting marriage rates. While the 1950's saw a 20% average divorce rate, the 1970's more than doubled that rate, with an astonishing 50% divorce rate. That's one out of every two marriages ending in divorce! It's no coincidence that marriages and families began to suffer after women started demanding equality during that Second Wave of Feminism in the '60's.

And of course we all know, and statistics show, that children exposed to broken family lives are much more likely to reproduce that brokenness in their own lives one day, having never seen the importance of commitment modeled for them. It's a vicious cycle that will continue until someone strong enough steps up to the plate, goes against the mold, and breaks the chains.

Decades later, in our new millennium, we haven't seen a decline in the divorce rate either, though predictions are that future statistics will show a deceiving decline, only due to couples' hesitancy to marry in the first place.

Another staggering statistic is that of women in the workplace, which only further reinforces the fact that the Feminist Movement was the catalyst of destruction among families.

Today, women make up almost half of the labor force in the United States. While three out of four families in 1960 had a stay at home parent (almost always the mother), now three out of four families have both parents working.

Furthermore, in over 65% of all households today, women are either an equal or majority source of income for the family.

God created woman as a suitable helper to man. He did not create her to take over man's responsibilities and demand equality in the Garden, *or* the workforce.

Another devastating result of the Feminist Movement is that women demanding the same rights and responsibilities as men have confused the sacredness of gender altogether. We are now a nation raising girly boys and manly girls, and having completely trashed the genders God gave us, we've unknowingly opened up a new door for further destruction of our already broken children, in a newer fad known as 'gender confusion'.

Our marriages and families are suffering now more than ever, and yet women everywhere resist the solution to the problem, all because we've been told by a bunch of broken women that we are worth more than what God created us for.

Stop and think about that!

I'll say it again, **"be not like dumb driven cattle!!"**

Open your eyes ladies. We were created in love, for a purpose, and with far more worth than any of us can comprehend.

That brings us full circle to that second point made in Chapter 1: We were created *second* to man, *for* the man.

So for argument's sake, let's assume that we can all agree that we were created *by God - second* to man, *for* man.

…what do we do with that?

So glad you asked.

Buckle your seat belts, girls, because this ride to success is going to be a bumpy one.

THREE

Jagged Little Pill

You know when you're sick, and the doctor tells you to take medicine that you just really don't want to take, but you know it will help make you well, so you take it?

Kind of like the chemotherapy rounds my mom had to take for breast cancer. She *really* didn't want to watch that medicine drip through that sterile tube right into her beat up body every three weeks, because she *knew* it would only be a matter of time after leaving the treatment center before she felt the nasty side effects that came along with having to have chemo. But she bravely refused to play the victim.

Instead, she took a deep breath, and did what was necessary to *ensure* that her cancer would never come back again.

Drip. Drip. Drip.

Consider this your chemo.

And your cancer - your troubled marriage or family.

Don't play the victim.

Don't delay the treatment.

Swallow the jagged little pill I'm about to give you with *confidence* that it will kill that cancer, once and for all.
And the pill is….

Submission.

Ugh. The very *word* sends chills down the spines of women everywhere.
It's a number one eye-roller, brow-furrower, book-closer.
But to those who want a successful marriage and thriving family, it is the KEY.
This one little frightening, infuriating, unbelievably frustrating word is the key. It's your first action. So all of you ladies who stuck with me to find the first 'to-do', here it is!
Submit.
Is it everything you imagined!? Not so much, huh.

Remember, I said this wouldn't be easy. Just trust me.

I'm sure you're wondering what this word, *submission*, actually entails.
Let me tell you how it works for me.

I mentioned in the forward how I am an opinionated person. I, like most people, by fleshly nature, assume I'm always right. I don't mind a challenge - in fact I thrive on one (... just ask my poor family!); and, I don't mind telling you what I think.
Now most of those things are good qualities, if used in godly ways.
Confidence and willingness to fight for what is right are both qualities that Jesus wants us to possess in order to share His gospel effectively and make disciples of all men.
But, just as an opinionated, confident employee knows his place with regard to his boss, an opinionated, confident woman should know her place with regard to her man, and if she doesn't, she must *learn* her place in order to achieve success in her family.

Now I was blessed with a dad that always encouraged his daughters to prepare for submission to her husband, so I may have it slightly easier than you. But only VERY slightly. Submission, even if prepared for, is HARD.

The best advice my dad ever gave me was to choose my husband wisely. He promised if I did that, I wouldn't have an issue with submission.

I wish I could say that I followed that advice, but I'd be lying if I did.

Of course I *thought* I was choosing wisely at the time, being so in love and obsessed with my man… but in retrospect, my heart was guiding me instead of my head. My feelings won out over my wisdom. Thanks be to God alone that He got ahold of both me and my husband and graciously saved, humbled, and convicted us in the ways that He has.

Failing to choose a spouse wisely happens all too often, though. Women (especially) get caught up in the idea of being 'in love', and fail to seriously consider the future objectively.

So, if you're reading this book with the preconceived misconception that I have a successful marriage because I somehow managed to make all the right relationship decisions along the way, relax. I can assure you that's not anywhere near the truth, and I can relate to many of you, because I didn't choose my husband wisely or consider my future objectively (at all) either. But God had plans (and of course grace) for my marriage, and while I didn't take that piece of advice that my dad gave me, I *did* remember it, and have come to understand the importance of what I failed to do.

Now *please* understand that what I've said here is NOT a slam against my husband. He is the best thing that's ever happened to me, outside of my salvation. Instead, it's a slam against ME.

I didn't do my job in properly preparing myself for marriage and ALLLLLLL of the different obstacles that come along with it! It is 100% *only* by the grace of God that we have grown into the successful family that we are today. And I believe part of the reason He so graciously allowed that to happen is so that you could read the very words that you are reading right now.

I know that while I wasn't considering my future, God was. He allowed our relationship to thrive, and prepared the unique circumstances we have experienced in order to mold us into voices for His glory.

I did all the wrong things, and He did all the right ones. He knew the calling He would place in my life to write this book for *your* benefit, and I believe that He was gracious and merciful to me, not only because He loves me, but because He loves *you!*

What I write to you in these pages has been prayerfully considered, and edited time and time again, at the direction of the Holy Spirit; so I have total confidence in this material.

I'll caution you though, in reminding you that this book is a guide for a successful marriage and family, not a perfect one. Marriage is hard, no matter who you are, but facing hard times doesn't mean you can't have success!

Furthermore, though, this slam against myself here is a testament to you that this submission thing really can work (no matter if you happened to have 'chosen wisely' or not). Just remember, though, it was only through my choice to submit to God first, and my husband second, that our success was achieved.

I can say with complete security to you that my husband is my leader. I submit fully to him, and in turn, he *wants* to (and does!) make my life absolutely wonderful.

Now don't go thinking our lives are, or ever have been, perfect. I'll say it again - marriage is hard, and at times ours has been too. But we've clung to each other, and more importantly to the Word of God.

I'll tell you a secret, too. Even though my dad prepared his daughters to submit to their husbands, it took a little trial and error (or maybe a lot) before I realized what true, total submission meant.

You can't just 'halfway' submit to your husband… trust me. I tried that toward the start of our marriage, really without even realizing it. I was (and still am!) head over heels in love with this guy, but I was (and still am!) headstrong and opinionated. That made submission a fight for me, because even though I wanted to please my man with every fiber of my being, I still wanted to do some things the way I thought they should be done. Over time, I realized though, that the more control I actually gave my husband, the more powerful and responsible he felt, because I wasn't fighting him for it - I was trusting him.

And over time, *he* realized that too - that I was putting all my trust and faith in him in every situation, and was giving *him* the control, the power, and the responsibility.

Knowing that I put my faith in *him* makes him want to succeed in whatever area I give him control of.

Knowing that I am trusting *his* judgment enough for him to consider my thoughts and feelings and still have the final say makes him puff up his chest a little more.

And knowing that our family depends solely on *his* salary alone provides him with a satisfaction you can't even begin to match, as he knows he is able to provide for the needs of our growing family *all* by himself (through God's provision of course).

Seeing my husband, marriage, and entire family thrive actually makes me *want* to submit. Really.

And hey, let's look on the bright side - if I'm not making the decisions, I can't be held responsible for the flops!

Don't get me wrong, it's still an internal battle each time I make the conscious effort to surrender my will to his (perhaps better said *His*), but I just think of the bigger picture, and how God can and *will* honor my submission to my husband (and how He already *has*). And then I realize what seemed important to me in the first place really isn't.

So my dad was right. Choosing your husband wisely helps ensure that you will end up with the right kind of man - one who won't take advantage of your choice to submit.

But I'm proof that choosing to submit to your husband without having wisely considered the seriousness of marriage *can* allow you to see the same success in your marriage and family.

It may be a long shot, but I'm assuming that some of you reading didn't 'choose so wisely' either. Maybe you thought you did at the time, but now it isn't working out exactly like you thought it would.

Maybe you're not even married yet; or perhaps you're on your third marriage and have already decided once and for all that you are never going to answer to *any* man, ever again.

Regardless of your current situation, your past, or your hard headedness - submission is still the *key* to your success. Most importantly, submit to God. He will guide you in the specifics on submission in your marriage better than I ever could!

And before you write off submission, just remember that God is the God of the impossible, and there is no lost cause to Him. All He desires is a willing heart from you in order to showcase His ability to work miracles in your life (and that really goes for anything, not just submission!).

And before you get too big for your britches thinking your husband is undeserving of your submission, remember what Christ did for you on the cross. None of us are deserving of anything other than Hell, yet we've been offered the gift of eternal life in Heaven if we receive Jesus as our Savior. Does your husband deserve your submission? Absolutely not. Should you submit anyway? Yes.

Is that to say that I suggest marriage be some domineering relationship between a master and his slave? Read this clearly: ABSOLUTELY NOT! While man was designed to rule over woman (like it or not), that command is not to be misused. Instead, marriage is intended to be a partnership that lovingly balances the strengths and weaknesses of both the husband *and* the wife. Just because wives are to submit to their husbands doesn't mean that their husbands never allow them to control anything. For instance, a good Christian friend of mine is far more financially savvy than her husband, so she controls the family's finances. Does that mean she's failing to submit? Not at all. On the contrary, she's a very submissive wife, who has arranged with her husband (who is her leader) that she should be in charge of the family's money - that *he* earns! It's actually a beautiful picture of a godly marriage! A man who assesses the workload, recognizes his weaknesses, and appropriately and lovingly delegates responsibility to his *helper* is exactly the kind of husband God wants him to be; and a woman who is willing to yield her control to that man, while at the same time making herself willing and available to meet the specific needs he delegates to her, is just that kind of wife God wants *her* to be.

So yes, marriages are partnerships, but partnerships in which wives submit.

For some of you scratching your heads right now, wondering just how all of this would work with *your* husband, don't be overwhelmed. Even without knowing your specific situation, I know that submission is the key. God may lead you to get creative in your submission, depending on your unique situation, and it may start small and grow over time. That's OK. That's good. Let God lead *you*. Just make sure you follow Him.

With all that said, though, before moving on, I want to pause here for a minute, because there may be *someone* out there reading this right now whose husband is physically abusive, and in no mental or emotional position of safely handling his wife's submission.

So let me stop here and make this point very clearly:

IF you are in a physically dangerous, abusive marriage, you **do** need to protect yourself and your children first and foremost, bottom line.

Once you've done that, *then* focus on submitting. Despite your unbelievably difficult circumstances - ones that I can not even *begin* to fathom, let alone counsel you on - let me encourage you to trust that God has allowed you to walk this road for a reason. Ask Him to help you, and trust Him that He will. Trust that He will provide a way for you and your loved ones, and surrender your life to Him.

His plan for you is not to harm you. Jeremiah 29:11 actually promises the opposite. His plan is to give you a hope and a future. Trust that and lean on Him.

As for submission, the specifics for your situation are going to have to come from God alone; but follow His lead. You're the likely candidate for creative submission that will start *very, very small*, and that's ok. God can work all of this for good, if you will let Him.

Bottom line, submission shouldn't override personal protection; *however,* it is still the key to your ultimate success.

No, I don't claim to be an expert on abusive relationships, and should you find yourself in this situation, I would encourage you to seek out those people who are trained to help you work on the specifics of your family's circumstances. With God's grace and your devotion to Him, even *you* can still yield the fruit of success, even in *your* marriage and family, all for His glory.

Let's continue.

Submission, by definition, is 'the action or fact of accepting or yielding to a superior force, or to the will or authority of another person'.

Lots of scary words in that definition, especially when considering submission to your husband - I hear ya.

Yielding. Superior. Authority.

Your first instinct is to resist all of this! But don't.

Accept it. Don't resist. Accept.

Yes, as with most issues, acceptance is the first hurdle to jump in the obstacle course of submission.

Read this clearly: If you *never* accept, you will *never* have true success, because you will always, in the back of your mind, feel entitled to more.

In fact, if you refuse to accept the decision of submitting to your husband, you might as well chunk this book now, because there's no point in reading any further.

If you want success in your marriage - *true* success (happiness, peace, security, joy, etc.), then you *have* to accept submission.

Accept the Biblical role. Accept the historical statistics.

Surely you know that nothing worth having comes easily.

Accept the challenge, no matter how crazy it seems.

Accept submission.

Accepted? Good. Now onto hurdle #2: Embracing.

That's right, I want you to 'willingly and enthusiastically support' submission, with open arms. Like you do when you really hug someone! Cling to it tightly and affectionately, never desiring to let go!

OK, now you're surely thinking I'm psychotic! This book was a waste of money! Accepting that submission is right is one thing, but 'hugging' it, and openly supporting it?! Seriously??

That would make you weak! Insecure! Unrealistic!

I know these accusations well.

But forget what everyone else says. If you've learned anything in this book so far, you've learned that this is in actuality going to take a very *strong, secure, and real* woman to implement these changes and fight for her family.

Don't play the victim. Embrace submission.

Why? Because refusing to embrace will prevent your success.

You can sweep the kitchen floor because it needs to be done. But if you don't embrace it - if you don't really commit to the need - you will not do the job to the best of your abilities. You will only do the job half way, which will result in frustration and defeat.

Frustration in the fact that you spent your valuable time doing something necessary, yet there are *still* crumbs on the floor - you know, around the baseboards, under the chairs you should have moved, and around the backside of the trashcan.

Seeing how your half hearted effort didn't truly accomplish the goal brings you to defeat. Seeing that you failed after choosing to rush through this responsibility leaves you realizing that you wasted valuable time and energy doing a job half way.

These feelings of frustration and defeat can cause you to wrinkle your brow (careful, it could get stuck like that!), or pitch a fit bigger than you'd care to admit. And sometimes people decide that since their efforts obviously failed them, they just need to pay someone *else* to come in and sweep.

See the parallel? Lots of people pay therapists and doctors to fix problems that they could have fixed themselves if they just put the time and energy into truly fixing the issues they were facing in the first place.

Compare that scenario of failure, though, to one of success.

In this case, the woman (let's say you) saw that the floor needed sweeping, and embraced her responsibility. She took out her broom, rolled up her sleeves, and got to work - fully committed, reaching for those baseboards, stacking all of the chairs on top of the table, and moving the trashcan to sweep behind it. While she didn't *enjoy* sweeping, now her floor is spotless and she feels a sense of accomplishment and success.

So... frustration and defeat? Or Accomplishment and Success?
Embrace.

But... *how?*
How do we embrace the fact that men are to be our 'masters'?
Yikes! Stop with the scary words!
It takes a real woman. Read on.

FOUR

No more WoPerDaughter

E mbracing submission takes a real *woman*.
A woman who isn't afraid to be called a woman. A woman who isn't intimidated, infuriated, or insecure of her God-given role to submit to a man.

We women must embrace submission by accepting who we were created to be.

Women who are bothered by the idea of submission have *something* holding them back, *something* that prevents them from embracing submission and living it out unashamedly.

Perhaps you are one of these women.

All too often, women who find fault with submission did not (or do not) have a positive male influence in their lives.

Many of you reading this book have experienced this.

Maybe you had a dad walk out on you.

Perhaps you became involved in a physically abusive relationship.

Maybe your husband had an affair.

Perhaps you can't relate to those examples, but I would venture to say that the overwhelming majority of women who are offended by the thought or suggestion of submission have had *some* kind of negative influence from a prominent male figure involved in their life at some point in time or another.

And considering that, it's no wonder that so many women have such a guard up.

See, women have certain needs just like men do, and when a man neglects or abuses a woman in his life in some way, it automatically puts her on the defense.
When a man walks out, a woman may vow to never fully trust a man.
When a man has an affair, a woman may vow to never let a man have all of her heart again.
When a man is abusive, a woman often decides that she better off alone, forever.

There are more examples, but you see the trend.
Negative male influences *understandably* affect women.

But, while none of us can change the past, we *can* overcome it.
Real women - strong women - who want change... who want success... *have* to address the underlying issues that prevent us from embracing submission. Otherwise, we will never achieve success.
Bluntly speaking, we *have* to be willing to set those issues we have aside and 'get over it'.

That's the point of this chapter - to get over it.

Regardless of our past, let's make the conscious decision to let it go. Move on. Get over it. Let's quit playing the victim - even if we *are* the victim.
We can champion over our obstacles by refusing to let our past (or present) outlook on men dictate us.
Or... we can give into defeat by continuing to push for gender equality in support of feminism and insist that submission is beneath us.
The choice is ours.

So what will you do?

Choose submission.
Use it. It can work.
It scares us. It frustrates us. It pains us.
But it can work.

Chances are, if you are offended right now, you likely fit the aforementioned criteria, and that's ok. That's not a slam, it's just a fact. It's what you do *now*, though, that determines your success.
You can put this book down and keep doing things the way you always have, or you can fight the urge to burn these pages and keep reading, determined to achieve the success you know you want for your family.

Remember, I promised that it would not be easy!

Ok, so for argument's sake (again), let's assume that we all agree to embrace submission by choosing to 'get over' the idea that it's beneath us, for the sake of our marriage and family.

But... now that we are done fighting the idea of submission, and we've agreed to embrace it, exactly how do we submit?

Glad you asked.

Now, the specific submissive relationship I'm going to focus on here is submission to your husband. Of course the Bible says children are to obey, or submit, to their parents; and it also tells us that, as Christians, we are to submit our lives to God. But, again, seeing as this book is designed to bring about successful marriages and families, the submission we're talking about is directed at wives (or future wives!) with regard to their husbands.

So with that in mind, wives... while I can't answer *specifics* on how *you* should submit to *your* husband, I *can* make some suggestions to figure out those specifics for yourself.

Start by **serving him.** Serving your husband gets you thinking, which will help you work out your specifics of submission. Consider your hubby's realistic *wants* and then, to the best of your abilities, give them to him.

What's his favorite meal? Cook it for him.

What's his favorite candy bar? Surprise him with it.

Does he drink coffee in the morning? Wake up 10 minutes early and make it for him so that he doesn't have to.

Find small ways to serve him, and take advantage of *every* opportunity you have. This can be overwhelming, as you certainly need a break sometimes too - especially if you're a mama! But give it your all and you will be surprised by how your loving, random acts of kindness may inspire him to *want* to please you too.

After awhile, you might just find *your* favorite candy bar hidden somewhere! So consider his wants, and then serve him.

And in thinking of ways to serve him and put him first, you will eventually begin to see different ways that you can yield control to him in different situations. And if for some reason, you still find yourself struggling to come up with ways to submit, don't worry, I've included some suggestions for you here!

(And here's a hint - while the specifics of submission will vary from one marriage to the next, **ALL** of the following suggestions can and should be implemented in some way in every marriage. That means you can't skip any of them!)

Support him.

If he has an idea, even if it seems totally crazy to you, go with it.

Even if you think it's gonna *flop*. Even if you *know* it will.

Furthermore, when it does flop, *never* say "I told you so". *Never* bring up failures. *Never* make him feel ridiculous. Remember that if you're submitting, you are acknowledging that he is your leader, so allow him to make the decisions, good or bad, and be willing to go down with the ship. You just might be surprised when it stays afloat!

This doesn't mean you're not allowed to have input in your decisions as a couple. It simply means that ultimately, *he* makes the call.

Feed his ego.

Do you love him? Tell him! Over and over and over. You can't say it too much.

And if you're no longer sure of your *love* for him... find something that you *like* about him and tell him that instead (Come on, you can find something. And no, you can't tell him that you like his wife!).

Regardless of your depth of love at this very moment, submission by feeding his ego is important.

Tell him he's attractive. Oogle over his muscles. Brag about his strengths! This will boost his confidence and make him happier, and will ultimately work for *your* benefit, and that of your family! Remember, God created woman *for* man - implying there was a need. He *needs* you - your love, your approval, your satisfaction in him. Give it to him!

Don't deny him anything you are able to give him.

If he asks you to do something and you are capable of doing it, then do it (so long as it doesn't go against the Bible!) and do it with a *good attitude*. And yes... this includes intimacy too - even after a long and exhausting day! Your willingness in all things will not go unnoticed.

Respect him, especially in front of other people.

He's your man, so don't belittle him and make him out to be ignorant, to him *or* to *anyone else*. After all, you chose him. What does that say about you?

I know what some of you are thinking right now... you didn't choose *that*. You didn't choose him how he is right *now*.

Wrong.

Unless you had an arranged marriage - highly unlikely - you chose him. What you meant to say is that you had no idea when you chose him that this is what you were going to get.

Doesn't matter.

It's what you got.

I don't care how mean he is, how lazy he is, how fat he is, how rude he is, how irritable, selfish, annoying, ignorant, or ridiculous he is. He is your man. And you chose him.

So respect him.

Even if he's not around to *hear* it, it's still disrespectful to tear him down to others. Instead, talk about him in encouraging ways. You'd be surprised at how doing this will elevate *your* opinion of him!

But.... what if you find your marriage seriously struggling, to the point of divorce?

What if respect right now is the furthest thing from your mind because of what he did to you? What if he just doesn't deserve it! I'll remind you of the cross.

Keep in mind that respect comes in many different forms.

Sometimes, in particular cases, your respect for your husband is actually your silence. For example, you refuse to broadcast your husband's shortcomings to the world. Or maybe you choose not to vent to a certain gossipy friend after a marital fight. Or maybe, in some cases, it means you just don't respond to an idiotic comment from your man with what automatically pops into your head.

Respectful silence is *very* underrated.

Now, facing difficult relational issues alone is not what I'm advising. In fact, on the contrary, having a friend or family member who you can open up to about your struggles can be a blessing to both you and that person. But needing to vent, craving some advice from a friend, or just needing a shoulder to cry on doesn't mean you can't still show respect. You just have to do those things in appropriate ways.

(Hint - updating your FaceBook status for the world to see you belittling your husband for the sake of venting is NOT showing respect!)

If you find yourself needing to talk to someone, find someone who you *trust* - but more importantly, someone who you *know* will offer you *positive* feedback and helpful suggestions. Respecting your husband doesn't mean that you can never ask others for advice; it just means you choose carefully your confidant and the issues you discuss.

Respecting your husband also doesn't mean you always have to agree with him, but it *does* mean that you choose to handle your differences in a mature way, with the willingness to support *him* and his decisions at the end of the day.

Do things his way.

Do the little things each day the way *he* wants to do them. Even insignificant decisions that don't require your 'support' can and will show him you're choosing to submit.

Maybe he prefers to eat dinner at 7:00 p.m. instead of your desired time of 6:30 p.m. Perhaps he likes 2% milk more than your preference of 1%. Or maybe he wants to take a shortcut on the way to the beach (even if you KNOW it's not a shorter way!).

Whatever it is, give him the reins and let him take control... even if you *really* want differently, *or* think you know better!

Doing these 'less important' things *his* way (without complaining!!) will show him that you are choosing to let him lead you each day, which will make him feel important. And making him feel important will ultimately lead to his desire to please you.

Ask him for help.

This can be difficult sometimes, because it makes us feel inadequate, but trust me - it's important. Request his physical assistance, comprehension, and advice in difficult situations, not just 'chores'. For instance, don't just ask his physical assistance in changing the baby's diaper or cleaning off the table. Ask him to lift a heavy box for you, or check your oil!

Knowing that you need him for something other than an extra pair of hands will empower him and make him feel valuable.

And don't stop there - ask him for help sometimes even if you *don't* need it... simply to make him *feel* needed!

These suggestions are not at all meant to demean or belittle you. We've already established that you have unmatchable worth, remember!

And, sure, they may seem ridiculous at first glance, but embracing submission in these ways show that you are a secure woman.

Again, each of you will have to figure out the specifics involved in each of these areas, according to your lives and your relationships.
That's the *easy* part.

Then... you actually have to *do* it.

Without complaining.

(Go ahead and cringe!)

Bottom line is, you have to treat submission like it's your **job.**

Perhaps you already have a job.
Consider your responsibilities at work. Of course you don't like all of them, but they are necessary. And complaining doesn't change the fact that these responsibilities still need to be accomplished. Over time, you've likely learned that complaining about things doesn't get you anywhere, whereas a positive attitude does. People notice when you have a positive attitude - especially when the work is tough.

So apply that to your new job of submission, and without complaining, make this new job *the most important.*

Trust me... it *will* be worth it.

Embracing submission also means that you should surround yourself with positive, supportive people who will encourage you in your quest for family success. Find a friend, family member, or pastor that will sincerely help hold you accountable to your acceptance and embracing of submission.
A few years ago, I ran a half marathon, and trained for six months leading up to that race; and let me tell you - training was hard! But... I embraced it, because I knew if I didn't, I would give up. I met with a group of girls three times a week to run. We supported each other and encouraged each other in our quest for a successful race. And guess what?
I achieved my personal goal of running the entire half marathon!
But I couldn't have done it without those girls.
Accountability and encouragement is what will help keep you going!

All through my childhood, my daddy always quoted his sister's joke that society will soon reach a point where we can't even say the word *woman* because our world will be too politically correct, and as a result, would be offended that the word *man* appears in *woman*. He continued that, in an attempt for political correctness, we will one day drop '*man*' from *woman* and instead insert '*person*', thus creating the new word 'woperson'. Of course... we will then have to consider that the word *son* appears in the new word 'woperson', and would still favor the man. So we'll obviously have to replace the *son*, with *daughter*, so as not to discriminate against women; and will in turn form the brand new word: *woperdaughter*.

Remember the old saying 'There is truth in jest'?

Come on ladies, no more *woperdaughter*.
Let's get over being offended by gender inequality and put the man back in the driver's seat where he belongs.
Let's submit.
Let's save our families.

FIVE

Homemade Bread is Better

Picture this with me: a big, puffy loaf of piping hot, freshly cooked, homemade bread cooling on a big wooden cutting board on the kitchen counter - the delicious aroma filling up the entire house. Mmmmmm. I can smell it now.

Ok, now picture this: a partially smashed loaf of bread wrapped in bread wrap, tied with a broken bread tie, thrown up on the top shelf of the pantry, that you bought in a **BOGO** deal at the grocery store two weeks ago.

Now.... both are edible, but which bread would you rather have?

I'm guessing there aren't too many people that will disagree with the title of this chapter, right? Generally speaking, homemade bread (or homemade anything!) is better.

Remember the well-known phrase about having to go to work: "I've got to go win the bread".
It's all about the bread.

Men and women across the globe head out for work every single morning to 'win the bread'. To pay the bills. To provide for their family's wants and needs.

What the vast majority of people don't realize, though, is that they are 'providing for their families' at the *cost* of their families. They've deceived themselves about what is necessary provision for their families, and are working themselves silly; all for another loaf of smashed up, store bought 'bread'.

Follow me here - we've jumped from bread as a food to a metaphor of the average American family.
The *average* family does not experience the success that is compared to the puffy loaf of freshly cooked homemade bread.
Let me explain why.
According to U.S. census studies, statistics showed that in 2013, more than 95% of average American families saw both father *and* mother in the workplace.
Also in 2013, national psychology reports revealed that up to 50% of American marriages end in divorce - the same statistic we recall of the year 1970.

Think back to the Second Wave of Feminism that began in the '60's. Do you remember how the fight for gender equality during that time encouraged women to join the workforce? Isn't it interesting how the divorce rate went up (and clearly stayed up) only *after* women started working?
It's no coincidence.
It's cause and effect.

And keep in mind that just because 50% of marriages end in divorce, that doesn't automatically classify the other 50% of marriages as 'successful'. Many people stay together, legally, these days 'for the kids', yet they've emotionally checked out. They fight like cats and dogs, step out on their spouses, and spend increasing amounts of time at work in an attempt to make up for the success their family lacks some other way.

So what's the common denominator here? Hang onto your hats, girls.

Statistically speaking, it's working women.
(Insert your 'Oh no she didn't!' here).

Ok, so IF the problem is working women, then... what do I suggest?
If you're a working mom, do I suggest that you quit your job today so that your family can experience success?

Oh boy.

Alright now, calm down... I'm in no position to suggest that women everywhere just quit their jobs; nor am I in a position to promise a woman that should she choose to do that, she would absolutely see success in her marriage and family.
While *statistics* might suggest it, *I* don't encourage *any* woman to just up and quit her job without *serious* prayerful consideration.

For instance, perhaps you're a single mom, and your children depend on you to work. You should!
Or perhaps you're a single woman who is dependent upon herself. That's good! You should work, and strive for excellence (however, you should still maintain gender inequality, as challenging a man's position as leader in the workplace can easily lead to a dangerous feeling of unrest and entitlement - which is what started the Feminist Movement in the first place).
Or maybe you're absolutely sure that God called you to your particular profession. Then, by ALL means, work, woman!

All this chapter is here for is to present statistical, historical facts about women in the workforce and show you the truth about what it has done to the average family. Consequently, my prayer is that this information will encourage women to evaluate their own lives to see if, in fact, homemade bread is better for their family, as it's proven to be in the past.

Read this chapter knowing that I have very close friends and family who are women in the workforce, and I'm thankful for each one of them.
I also do business with plenty of women in the workforce, and am particularly thankful for ones like my OB/GYN who delivered my babies, or their pediatrician who helps keep them well.

I utilize the services of women in the workforce on a regular basis!

I'm not writing these words to pass judgment on working women, regardless if they're moms or not. My goal, instead, is to present facts and provoke thought.

I don't want working women to get offended at the suggestion that they shouldn't work! I want working women out there to be encouraged that there may be a reason, and more importantly a solution, for the problems their families may be struggling with.

Maybe you're one of those working moms who wouldn't consider her family to be struggling with her working, and perhaps that's true. Perhaps it's not God's desire for you to quit working, as He very well may have you right where He wants you for now.

I'd still encourage you to read ahead though, and really consider the material presented, the current state of your marriage and/or family, and most importantly, what *God* truly wants for your family. *Many* women will try to justify their own desires by saying they believe God has called them to their job, when, in reality, He hasn't. There's a difference in God allowing someone to choose their profession, and calling them to a specific place for His glory.

Just make sure that you're not one of the ones trying to justify her own wants - not for my sake, but for *your own*.

Now all this 'working women stuff' is *mainly* directed at those of us women who are *mothers*, even more specifically, mothers of children roughly ages 18 and under.

That said (and exceptions and extenuating circumstances aside) let's look at the damage that a typical family with children can see from a mother in the workplace, and the different reasons why she's likely there.

Take a minute and ponder with me *why* most American families see both father and mother working? The answer is pretty obvious, right?

The overwhelming majority of people defending their decision for both mother and father to work argue that both incomes are needed to 'win the bread' - to pay the bills.

Alright, fair enough.

So my next question would be... *exactly what are your bills?*

(Uh oh, now she's getting way too personal!)

Did you know that the average young couple in America with two children *needs* to make $100,000 this year to live?
This salary allows said family to make a hefty house payment on a roughly $200,000 home, one car payment, one student loan payment, credit card payment(s), contribution(s) to 401K plans etc., *and* pay other necessary bills each month (power, water, groceries, etc).

A $100,000 annual income - now that's quite a substantial amount of money to bring in for a young couple! But.... it *is* necessary in order to pay *those* bills!

And all of those bills are necessary.
Right?

Ready for another bubble to be popped?
POP.
Wrong.

Not even *half* of those bills are necessary, but we've allowed ourselves to become convinced that they are.
We've allowed society to confuse our needs from our wants, and have convinced ourselves that we would be totally lost without certain materialistic possessions.
It's the way of the world to have the nice house, the new cars, the credit cards, the clothes, the entertainment, the gadgets. All of those things are now overwhelmingly considered 'needs'. So it's no wonder that iPhones and PlayStation's, BMW's and suburb living, Louis Vuitton and Oakley run up American's *necessity* to make $100,000.

And we just blindly follow society, "as an ox goes to the slaughter, or as one in fetters to the discipline of a fool, until an arrow pierces through (our) liver; as a bird hastens to the snare, so (we) do not know that it will cost (us our) life."
Proverbs 7:22-23 makes it pretty clear the high cost that comes from following the dumb, driven cattle.
And our *families* are paying the price.

And of course, with both father *and* mother working so as to meet the 'needs' of our family, arrangements have to be made for the children, as no one is available to raise them for sake of paying the bills.

What's worse is that many women today have convinced themselves that they "could never" raise their own kids. They don't even *want* to.

Did you hear that? Many women today don't even want to 'fool with' raising their own children! They want to do as little as possible with the precious lives that God has entrusted them with, because their kids 'drive them crazy', or they 'don't have the patience', or simply because the thought of being with their children all day long is just 'exhausting' or 'stressful'.

So, daycares and public school systems are embraced, and we just buy right into the lies that these public institutions will be more beneficial and educational for children than the ever decreasing alternative of raising and teaching children in the home.

We make excuse after excuse to justify our 'bigger, better, & me' mentality, and all we've done is created this deserving nature for ourselves and our children, that has in turn destroyed the success of our families.

I actually had a friend who once told me that she *wished* she could stay home with her two children, but that she and her husband couldn't afford for her to because they had to buy a new car so that their kids would be able to travel safely on their way to daycare.

Hello!? That makes no sense!

She and her family, like so many others, were eating smashed up, store bought bread.

What I also found out later was that, while they seemed like a happy family on the outside, they were falling apart at home. Both my friend and her husband were working full time and each understandably stressed from their own job. Consequently, they only spent a fraction of their day together with their children 'as a family' - which was equally as stressful. Instead of (relatively) peaceful mornings at the breakfast table together, they were running around getting everyone ready to leave by 7:00 am; and instead of pleasant afternoons, when 5:30 pm rolled around, they found themselves arguing about dinner and the kitchen mess. And relaxing evenings? Ha - forget it! Instead they had to vacuum, clean the toilets, walk the dog, bathe the kids, brush their teeth, and get them in the bed. Their intimate life was suffering, they had little to no patience, little to no peace, little to no happiness. But hey - they were together, and their kids were safe in the new car on the way to daycare.

I just can't help but wonder... is that worth it?
Is all that stress and frustration worth the cell phone? The new car? The big house?

What many couples don't realize is that all too often, those pressures, stresses, and frustrations continue to build and never get better... and then one day, it's too late.
Husband and wife 'just don't love each other anymore' and are 'better off apart'.
And in steps the demon of divorce, along with more lies from society about being stronger and better off without that frustrating spouse.

And then we throw out the old store bought bread.

What's saddest is that the poor children of a splitting family see the stability that they once knew crash down before their eyes, teaching them not to have confidence in anything other than themselves, teaching them that commitment is not important, teaching them that it's OK to do what they want to do if it makes them happy. Because 'they deserve it'.
It's no wonder that we see increasing teen pregnancies, STD's, drug addicts, alcoholics, arrests, divorce, violence, and the like.

We are (as a whole) allowing the world to raise our children to become another statistic!

We have to forget society's insistence on what we 'need'.
We *must* refocus our sights on what's truly important, make the necessary cuts, and get back on track.

And by the way, I'm here to tell you that a young family (of *five*) in America does not NEED to make $100,000 to survive, nor do both parents NEED to work.

A typical starting salary for a middle class man is roughly $30,000, and with the right cuts (the Louis Vuitton's, the BMWs, the iPhones, etc), and the right monthly budget, a young family of five can not only survive, but thrive *and save*, on that income - debt free.

How do I know that?

Because I lived it.

Having lived within our small means was hard, but was so incredibly beneficial for us.

Living within your means is not always easy, but from personal experience, it's incredibly rewarding to know that the really difficult sacrifices we have been willing to make have achieved (and continue to achieve) our family success.

I won't lie to you.. it takes work. A LOT of work.

It takes time.

It takes patience.

But that homemade bread is *so* much better, and *so* worth it.

SIX

Extra Pickles

I *love* Chick-Fil-A.

Not only is their food delicious, but their service is incredible! The employees maintain a pleasant attitude, almost always have a smile on their face, and never fail to go above and beyond your typical 'fast food' experience.

If you've ever been to a Chick-Fil-A, you know what I'm talking about; but on the chance you haven't, let me give you some examples of their superior service. Unlike some of their competitors, instead of yelling 'NEXT!', Chick-Fil-A employees always politely ask if they can 'serve the next guest'. In the same manner, they don't wait for you to come up to the front for a drink refill, but instead, take initiative to walk around the restaurant checking on their customers, asking if they can 'refresh your beverage'. They clean off the tables as soon as customers leave instead of waiting to be asked. They refill their condiment tables *before* they run empty. And they make sure there are always beautiful, fresh flowers on each table.

Oh, and listen to them the next time you thank them for something. Their response will be, without fail, "my pleasure".

It also just so happens that a Chick-Fil-A chicken sandwich is one of my favorite things to eat.

Fantastic service aside, there is just literally not another restaurant that makes a chicken sandwich as good as they do!

I have found, though, that there is *something* I can add to that delicious chicken sandwich that will make it even *more* enjoyable.

Extra Pickles.

In fact, I never order one without them now. Once I tasted that 'extra', I've never wanted to go back.

Don't get me wrong, it was good without them - even great. But those tiny little additions... those tiny little extras... they *make* the sandwich for me.

Now being the clever reader that you are, I'm sure you've picked up on the direction in which I'm going, right? Right.

So... what are the extra pickles for your marriage and your family?

What could be added to make those things even *better* than *good*?

Where the secret to success is submission, the secret to a *more enjoyable* success is selflessness.

Imagine yourself as that Chick-Fil-A employee, asking your husband "How can I serve you?"

Quit laughing!

This is meant to be serious!

How can you serve your husband? Your family?

How can you be selfless?

See, the interesting thing to remember here, is that, even though they are serving selflessly, each Chick-Fil-A employee has a personal goal in mind. They want a paycheck for themselves, which drives their selfless desire and willingness to serve chicken.

And you, too, have a personal goal in mind - a successful marriage and thriving family.

But just like that Chick-Fil-A employee, you have to be willing to *serve* in order to achieve your goal.

And just like that Chick-Fil-A employee, you have to serve *with pleasure*.

Does this mean you have to like everything you do? Not at all.

I would venture to say that the folks at Chick-Fil-A probably don't *like* taking out the trash, or cleaning the bathrooms, or even taking order after order after order. Yet they do each task with a positive attitude, and respond to each request or need as though it pleases them to meet it.

That's because their focus is on their ultimate goal, not each individual task. That perspective allows them to do each task, even those that are less than desirable, with some degree of legitimate pleasure.

So let's not only succeed, let's succeed with flying colors. Lets go above and beyond. Because, after all, *we* will reap the rewards too.

If you survived chapters 1 - 5, and swallowed that jagged little pill we called submission (and kept it down), then you're well on your way to success already, even if you can't see the results yet.

But in preparation for that success, I want you to ponder what 'extras' you could add to your marriage and family, through selflessness, to make that success even more enjoyable *to them* - and ultimately to *you too*!

What are the extra pickles that you can serve to them, with pleasure?

You know your family, not me... so I can't answer that question specifically for you either. But I can clarify what I mean by 'extras', by defining 'selflessness'.

To be selfless is to be more concerned with the needs and wishes of others than with one's own self.

So, be thoughtful. Do things for your husband and children that they would appreciate, and I don't mean *materialistic* things. It's easy to buy your kid a new toy, but selflessness is more genuine when *not* focused on materialistic things. So.. spend time with them. Give them compliments. Write them love notes. Play with them! Go where they want to go. Do what they want to do. Give them hugs.

Concern yourself with the needs and wishes of your family *more* than those of yourself.

Flip back to Chapter 2, and review the list of 'typical housewife responsibilities' that were found in magazines during the 1950's. These women were not only submissive; they were *selfless*. That's just another reason why an astonishing 80% of them had successful marriages and families!

They made a habit of giving extra pickles!
And you should too!

Think of it this way - will your family remember you as 'just another fast food restaurant'? Or will you be remembered as a *'Chick-Fil-A'*?

SEVEN

Remember the Future

My desire to please my family and continue the cycle of success we experience has me constantly contemplating our future. *...And* my past. We've all heard the saying 'we learn from our mistakes'. How true that is! And yes, *I've* learned from my past mistakes, and you can be sure I won't make the same mistakes again. But I want to go a step beyond that, as does my husband.

We want to prevent our children from repeating our past.

So, we raise them differently.

Many people have the hope (or delusion) that their children will not make the same mistakes they made, yet they're unwilling to make the necessary changes in their lives to prevent it from happening.

But if there is going to be positive change from one generation to another, somewhere along the way, chains have to be broken. New habits have to be formed. Drastic measures MUST be taken.

Otherwise, we can *hope* all we want, but our past mistakes will haunt us in the future, through our children - *and theirs.*

This isn't a new concept - it's an ignored one.

God even tells us this in Exodus 34:7b, when He says our mistakes will affect generations to come:
"yet He will by no means leave *the guilty* unpunished, visiting the iniquity of fathers on the children and on the grandchildren to the third and fourth generations."
That is... unless we change.

What are the chances of the alcoholic's son not drinking?
What are the chances that the promiscuous pregnant teenage girl will raise her baby to value virginity?
What are the chances that the busy CEO's children will make time for their future families?

Now I'll be the first one to say that God can change whoever He wants, whenever He wants, regardless of how they may or may not have been raised. I've seen it.
But if parents wouldn't stop at just 'learning from *their* own mistakes', more children would experience future *success* because of significant change, instead of guaranteed *heartache* that awaits them learning from *their* own mistakes.
It's a vicious cycle that *can* be avoided, though most parents just refuse to do the work required.

Let's assume, though, that *you're* different.
A little work doesn't scare you when you consider your children's future. If change is what it takes, you'll do it. But... where do you begin?

Enter, convictions.

Conviction, by definition, is holding a strong opinion or belief.
Pretty simple.
And it's not uncommon for us to form strong opinions and beliefs about certain issues, having learned from our past mistakes.
But we all know saying we believe something and acting on that belief are two very different things. If we truly hold these strong opinions or beliefs now, though, about any given issues that our children may face, why would we not do everything we could to make it easier for them not to struggle or fall into temptation?

Taking the necessary steps to follow through with a conviction, though, isn't easy - on the contrary, it's incredibly difficult.

But you guessed it... *following through* with your convictions is what WILL make a difference in your life, and the lives of your family... not just *having* them.

That's the problem with convictions - most people have them, but few follow through with them.

Most people would chalk convictions up to their conscience telling them that they 'shoulda, coulda, woulda' and then pay them no further attention.

Then there's some who understand the need, but the thought of change is far too overwhelming, and so they don't.

There are also those who might make slight adjustments in certain areas of their lives, with the good intention of helping their children succeed... but they're not willing to change *everything*.

And then there are some who are determined and committed to changing any aspect of their current life, no matter the cost, for the sake of their family; and *they* are the ones who will see true success.

Making significant changes in your life is extremely difficult, and can no doubt be frustrating when you don't see immediate results. We *all* have a problem with delayed gratification - and I'm the worst!

But what we have to realize is that - with any positive change - the *future success* is worth the *current pain*.

Convictions are great, but they're worthless without follow through.

Think of it this way: Jesus says to follow Him, right? Well, that implies He's doesn't just want us to stay where we are. He wants us to listen to what He says, and take action. We must physically move, if we want to be with Him. Otherwise, we've *heard* Him, but haven't *listened*.

We can't have selective hearing in our convictions. That defeats the purpose. God reveals things to us that He wants us to change for a reason. And your family is no different.

Submission is key to your success.

Selflessness is key to your abundant success.

And *following through* with your convictions is key to your future generation's success.

And all *three* keys must be used in order to experience abundant success in your marriage and family.

So, Mamas, consider your past. What things would you tell your younger self to do differently, in order to prevent heartache that you experienced in your own life?

Which of your past experiences would you encourage your children to relive? Which ones would you prefer they not touch with a ten foot pole? But don't stop at pondering all of this! Take action to that consideration, and make the necessary changes to ensure success for your children, regardless of how difficult that action seems!

Not only can it provide success for your kids one day, but it can save *you* significant stress! Think about it!

Parents who stop at *hoping* their kids will make better choices than they did spend a lot of time worrying that they won't. Especially the older those kids get!

But parents who *take action* can enjoy confidence in their children, knowing that the changes they implemented years before prevented not only their *exposure* to negative choices, but often their *desire* to make them too!

I'll stop here to address the common fallacy: "Well, you can't keep your kids in a bubble".

But here's what I say - "why not?".

If our bubble ensures that our kids aren't exposed to the things we don't want them exposed to, and if our bubble constantly reinforces the reasons why those things are harmful, it will reduce (if not prevent) their desire to do those things when it comes time for them to leave the bubble. What's more, the 'bubble' can be as big and as flexible as you prayerfully discern it should be!

So... what's the harm?

I say there's plenty more harm in not taking action.

We can set our kids up for success.

Or we can hope that they find it themselves.

Just consider that certain exposures *now* increase probable future heartache in many different ways.

Perhaps for your child... Perhaps for you.

Perhaps for both.

See, satan (my Mama taught me to give him a little 's' on purpose - it's one way to intentionally 'stick it to him'!) knows what exposures he can use to 'steal, kill, and destroy' your family.

You realize that's what he's trying to do, right?

Steal.

Kill.

Destroy.

Your family.

Your husband.

Your babies.

You.

Regardless of whether or not you realize it, you are in the middle of a battle against satan, and you need to *take extreme action* to keep him from harming your family.

Consider my own life.

I grew up in a very strict Christian family. We were at church every Sunday; there was never an alcoholic drink present in our home; my parents were (and still are!) happily married; we didn't even have cable because our TV was so restricted.

Believe me, my parents did everything they could think of to keep negative influences out of our home, so as to prevent me from making mistakes they may have made in their past;

But what I've learned first hand is this - zero negative exposure at home is great, but the unprotected exposure of the *world* is greater.

Despite my parents efforts at home, the unprotected influences of the world ended up leading me down some of the very roads my parents worked hard for me to avoid.

I look back on my life as a youth and younger adult and realize that, while you can't shield everything from your children, you can control a lot more of what they're exposed to when you're *with* them.

The mistakes I made in high school and college were a direct result of me being exposed to negative influences from my peers in the public arena, in the absence of my parents.

Now, don't misunderstand me - I am not suggesting my parents failed me, or failed to follow through with their own convictions. On the contrary, actually, I'm showing that they *did* follow, as God led them. That's the beauty of God's sovereignty that we will never fully understand. He chose not to convict them in all the same ways He has me and my husband, because had He enlightened them in certain areas, *I* would not have the opportunities and callings that I have today - the exact ones that He wanted *me* to have; to use; to glorify Him!

In fact, I fully believe that my parents raised me to the full extent that God led them to, so that He could use me to reach *you*! While it's certainly not my job (or ability) to convict anyone, it *is* my job (and ability) to be obedient to the callings God has given me, so that *He* can do the convicting, as He so desires. And I believe, with all my heart, that He desired for *you* to read *this* book, at *this* moment in your life, so that seeds of conviction could be planted in your own life, and so that you could be encouraged to follow them through for the benefit of His Kingdom.

Prayerfully reflecting on *my* past, present, and future allows me to be convicted in ways that may be different from you, and that's ok; however, I do believe with my whole heart that what I'm convicted of would be beneficial for other families, not just mine.

As stated before though, my convictions are pointless if I don't follow through with the necessary changes required, and yours are too.

So what are your convictions? Don't have any?
I challenge you to start thinking.
Start by thinking of your family. Your children. How important to you are they?
Would you do anything to guarantee them success - where it truly matters?
What negativity is your family exposed to, and how?
What are your past mistakes that you don't want repeated?
What significant changes are you willing to make to prevent negative exposure to your family?

Now will you *hope* for success, or *work* for it?

PART 2

Humbling Hurts.

So for Part 2 of this book, I've decided to get personal with you.

Our family has embraced and implemented the guidelines from Part 1 into our lives, and so I want to share with you some specific convictions that God has led me and my husband to in our decade of marriage.

Allow me to share - but first, let me reiterate that this part of the book is dedicated to sharing the things that *our* family has chosen to do, at the direction of the Lord.

We don't claim to be perfect, nor do we think we are better than those who choose to do things differently. In fact, the following pages were the most edited pages of this book. These were the ones that proved most difficult to write, and the ones that made me truly appreciate God's grace. The road to these printed pages left me beaten and bruised with a big old foot in my mouth OFTEN. As I wrote, and rewrote, and rewrote, I was truly humbled, and praise the Lord He left us too poor to publish this book until said humbling happened.

Yes, these following pages elaborate on our personal choices, but this is just simply a list of some of the ways *we* have chosen to raise *our* family, that have helped us achieve that much desired success!

So… here ya go…

After prayerful consideration, Biblical application, and reflecting on our past together, my husband and I have chosen to live *our* lives and raise our family in the following ways (in no specific order). Read on!

EIGHT

Letting God Build our Family

L et's jump right in, shall we?
So we let God build our family... great - but what does that mean exactly?

Glad you asked.

In a nutshell, we have learned that God knows best. Always. About everything.

And that includes our family.

Now at the beginning of our marriage, this topic wasn't even discussed. As I recall, we both knew we wanted children at some point, but that was about it. We didn't talk numbers, we didn't talk timeline, we just figured it would happen at some point 'later'. When WE got ready for a baby. Our minds were not on the things of God at all, because, well... we were lost. We cared about what we wanted to care about, and that included a future family - key word at that point, 'future'.

I took a daily birth control pill for a few years, and was content in doing so until I happened upon some research that made me question whether or not using the pill was ethical. See, even though I was not yet saved, I did have a moral compass, and had grown up in a conservative home, and, as a result, was passionate about being pro-life.

The information I'd come across explained that birth control pills affect the lining of a woman's uterus, and thus is considered abortifacient in nature. This proved problematic to my continuing to take the pill. Being pro-life and believing that life begins at conception, my husband agreed that my taking a pill with the knowledge that it could destroy an already fertilized egg by preventing it from attaching to my uterine wall was out of the question. So we simply began using natural means of birth control instead, and for a few years, that was as far as our conviction went.

As we continued to grow in our faith, though, we began to question whether or not just refusing the *pill* was enough. Along the way, we decided we were ready for kids of our own, and I found myself expecting our first child. We were excited about becoming parents, and the pregnancy ultimately pushed us to finally surrender to Christ as our Savior. As a result, over the next few years, as new parents, we hungered for the pure milk of Jesus, and saw Him really began working in our lives, which was so exciting.
Still, we kept coming back to the question of how much 'control' is too much anyway?

This thought ultimately prompted a few years where we truly felt God leading us to forgo ALL forms of birth control - and we have the four children in the span of six years to prove it!

What I didn't realize was that it was during these years that I began to take a judgemental approach towards others who weren't letting God build their families in the same way that we'd been convicted at that time. In retrospect, I guess I'd figured *we'd* arrived, and everyone else who called themselves a Christian should have arrived too.
How ridiculous.
While I still believe that all families *should* let God do what He wants, I thankfully have come to realize that maybe *I* was wrong to assume each family's callings and situations would be automatically the same as ours.

I also do still believe that certain forms of birth control are wrong, but I know now that I am not able to speak in absolutes about such a personal issue.

The writing on the wall for me came along with a health diagnosis that put me back on the birth control pill temporarily. How's that for ironic? After lots of praying, and multiple conversations with my doctor, I realized that this pill we were in such opposition to before could at that particular time help me be a better mother to the children God had already given me. Furthermore, we found that the pill isn't actually abortifacient in nature like we thought. The pill does affect the lining of a woman's uterus, yes - but it's more of a cause and effect type situation. The lining is thinned because ovulation is avoided, not in an effort to prevent fertilized eggs from attaching. Other forms of birth control are designed to be abortifacient, but as it turns out, it isn't actually fair to group the pill into that classification.

Assessing my health and this information from my doctor, we realized that maybe God was actually closing a door on more biological children at the time, so that He could perhaps add to our family in a different way. After all, we'd felt God call us to adopt from foster care a year prior to this diagnosis, and we'd since been approved by our local DFCS office, and were now just waiting on the Lord to bring us the right child(ren). Maybe He was shutting one door before opening another, all while humbling us in the process to make us look more like Him.

Here's the bottom line: We don't know what the Lord has planned for us, but we are grateful that He has shown us grace in this area; grace that we will now pay forward, for sure. And we're certain that the best thing for *any* family is to listen to God on this touchy subject. We are simply committed to trusting Him to build our family how He sees fit, however that may be. He's the One in control anyway, remember. Our responsibility is to trust and obey Him. His plans are always better than ours, and His grace is sufficient in our weakness. The Lord will provide.

Switching gears a bit, we understand that our decision to trust God to build our family how He sees fit is not popular or accepted - for a host of reasons. Biologically or not, adding children to our family doesn't always sit well with people. We aren't bothered by these opinions, though, because our trust is in the Lord.

From a financial standpoint (which we have found to be the #1 argument), no matter if we have four kids, or twenty, *God* is really the One who provides for our family. Therefore, the ever popular question of *'How will you afford all those children?'* doesn't rest on my husband's shoulders, it rests on God's. Looking through that lens helps us remember that if we are dependent on God to provide for us right now, why could we not be just as completely dependent on Him to provide for us later as a larger family, should He see fit to give that to us. If we're going to trust God to provide for us, we can't set limits on His ability.

For *that* reason, we don't believe that having or potentially adopting a lot of children means that we are in some way committing financial suicide. We depend on God for financial security, and no one else, and we believe that we can be good stewards with what He chooses to entrust to us, regardless of the size of our family.

The financial argument is only one from the host of other arguments that we have heard from those opposing our conviction of letting God build our family, but our response to all questions will always, ultimately, be the same: If God is planning our family, He will provide for our needs.

So for those who wonder how we plan on showing many potential children enough individual attention, we would say "If God is planning our family, He will provide for our needs." If He decides to bless us with ten kids, we wholeheartedly trust that He would provide for each child's individual need for our attention in the right ways.

For those who wonder how we would prevent too much responsibility from piling up on all these potential children, we would answer "If God is planning our family, He will provide for our needs." We would also say that too much responsibility is a matter of opinion. While laundry, dishes, cooking, cleaning, grocery shopping, babysitting, yard work, and other daily tasks would no doubt prove to be overwhelming for parents of any large family, we believe that having our children help accomplish those tasks (as needed) would actually be good for them. That doesn't mean that my husband and I would hand off our own responsibilities to our kids so that they could do all the work for us. Instead, what it means is that we would delegate the workload appropriately to our children, considering their ages and personalities, and then use those opportunities to teach them that being a part of any family means helping out when needed. Our kids would still be able to 'be kids', they would just 'be kids' with responsibilities.

The bottom line is that we don't believe that arguably 'hard' work for children is a reason not to have them!

As I said before, there are plenty of other questions people can come up with about how we would make all this work, but we still say, every time, "If God is planning our family, He will provide for our needs". That's just something we've realized over the years, and we're committed to trusting Him.

What we've also realized over the years with this particular conviction (and others!) is that God can place specific adjustments or additions to a basic conviction in seasons.

The end result of what our family will look like is really just a big question mark for us, but that's ok, because we know Who holds tomorrow. And for all we know, maybe the four biological children we have right now are the only ones God will give us. And if that's His choice, that's fine with us too! We are incredibly thankful for their precious lives!

In a nutshell, this entire subject of birth control is a touchy one, and there's not a cookie cutter mold that just everyone fits in to. It's not as black and white as 'this is right' or 'that is wrong', and so just like any conviction, I'd say the specifics of this personal subject for your family is best left to God. I'd just encourage you to seek His will in your life on this issue and follow through however He leads you, through seasons and twists and turns and unknowns! I can say from experience, He knows best!

NINE

Trusting God with our Money

As I mentioned in the last chapter, we are committed to trusting God to provide for us in every way, including financially. This trust in God to provide for us, though, doesn't mean that we have no financial responsibility.

Claiming to trust God to provide, while just sitting around on the couch waiting for Him to drop a check in our mailbox each month doesn't work. On the contrary, trusting the Lord to provide for us means that we are willing to use the physical and mental gifts He has given us to the best of our abilities in order to *bring about* His provision. In fact, we expect that the doors He will open for us will require us not only to work, but to work *hard* - to roll up our sleeves and get our hands dirty. We know that without our willingness to do that, we would hinder His provision.

Over the years, we've also learned that, while we may have the physical and mental abilities to excel in certain areas that would allow us a comfy financial cushion, God may call us to other places. Places that pay less. And that's ok.

65

Early on in our marriage, we lived a comfortable, relaxing, materialistic life. Every cent of what we made went to *us*, and our 'bigger and better' mentality. We found ways to justify every want we had into a financial need, and the double income we enjoyed made our spending habits more affordable.

I say *more* affordable, because ironically, it was during that time in our lives that we enjoyed the double income enough to run up credit card bills that we couldn't afford. And it was also during that time in our lives that we struggled to keep money in our savings account. And it's no surprise, of course, that during that time in our lives we weren't giving at all.

We could afford all of what we wanted and none of what we didn't.

We were stupid!

Thankfully, though, God revealed our stupidity to us in His perfect timing, and began painfully peeling away the layers of our materialistic onion.

It was a very messy process.

As we gave into God, we were embarrassed, humiliated, ridiculed, mocked, and humbled; but by the end of it, we were financially broken for Jesus. And through His grace alone, He led us to a place of no debt, consistent monthly contributions to our growing savings account, consistent monthly contributions to a growing retirement account, consistent monthly contributions towards quarterly stock purchases, and most importantly, consistent generosity towards His Kingdom each month. *All* on *half* the income that we started with.

I don't tell you that to boast about us. I tell you that to boast of *Jesus*! Who else could do all that, but Him!?

We learned first hand, through becoming financially broken for Jesus, to depend solely on *Him*, and He would provide for us in every way, often in miraculous ways!

Depending completely on God's leadership and provision has been incredibly rewarding, despite the difficulty of choosing to live within a small one income means, but after a few years of living that way, we became more and more content with our frugal lifestyle. Content enough for God to bless us further, by starting on peeling away at yet another onion: pride. And as if the materialistic onion wasn't painful enough, the pride one *really* proved painful! But God knew which one to peel first. He knew we had to be truly content with less, and truly committed to living within our means before He started on our pride.

Through some major humbling, God allowed us to stay in a place of lower income for awhile, until our perspective changed. See, we were living within our means now, but our perspective on lower income folks, in general, was still more of a judgemental one, as much as I hate to admit that. But God knew that leaving us where He did for awhile, and even providing blessings to us in ways we didn't necessarily like, would humble us where we needed to be humbled. We recognized this, though we didn't like it, but, still, we surrendered to His will in our finances. And, let me tell you, He is faithful. He showed us much grace over our lower income years, provided manna for us in our wilderness, and in the right time, began to prosper us, for His glory.

We are thankful for the financial struggles we have had, the tough lessons we have learned, and the provision God has given us, even through outlets we didn't necessarily care for, for whatever the length of their season. The lessons surely didn't come easily, or quickly, but I am thankful that God gave me new eyes through which to see others - others who were created in the same image of God that I was, and I'm thankful He's been faithful to prosper us through our surrender of our money and our minds to Him.

The bottom line in this conviction is that we have put our trust in God to provide for us financially by walking through the doors He opens for us, at His direction, and we will continue to depend on Him to open new ones in His timing.
We encourage everyone we meet to do the same!

TEN

Raising Our Little Children at Home

S urely, by now, you have gathered that, yes, we have chosen to raise our kids at home! It's not exactly something we're hiding.

The short of it is, we have seen the statistics (many of which have been shared with you), weighed the options, and decided that if the Lord saw fit to give *us* children to raise, *we* should raise them.

Regardless of the cost. Regardless of the sacrifice.

The cost. The sacrifice. THAT was (naturally) the hardest part for us. *Hearing* God tell us to raise our babies at home was easy. Our hearts heard Him clearly. End of story.

Acting on that calling was the hard part. The really hard part. But what good are convictions without follow through, remember?

Thankfully, we decided to follow God's calling and actually *do* what He told us to do, despite immense difficulty. We made serious cuts - as mentioned before, even sold our brand new house - to follow through with this conviction.

It goes against the mold of society, today, to raise your little children at home, rather than send them to daycare and eventually public school; but that's what we've chosen, through prayerful consideration, for our family. A good friend once shared something with me that she heard a pastor say about sending your children to daycare: "If you truly believe that your children are the biggest gifts God has given you, why would you place them in the care of someone earning minimum wage?"

This conviction of ours isn't meant to 'knock' daycares or minimum wage jobs.

God can use any job, including someone working in a daycare, earning minimum wage, to provide for needs and reach the lost. In fact, I am very fond of our church's daycare program, where children are taught from a Biblical worldview, and kids that may otherwise never hear the gospel are introduced to Jesus! While we have chosen for me to stay at home with our children, we are thankful that there are daycares available to be a positive influence to those that need it.

So, relax. We don't think daycares are evil. They're just not for our family.

This chapter is pretty short and sweet - we raise our children in our home. And school eventually becomes a part of that, but that's for another chapter. You'll just have to keep reading!

ELEVEN

Filtering Entertainment

O n the surface, this conviction is probably something most people agree with, at least for their children. For instance, not too many parents let their small children watch violent content. I think it's pretty safe to say that most people censor their kids' entertainment in some way, at least until they reach a certain age.

We've realized, though, that temptations from entertainment can come in all shapes and sizes, and can affect both children *and* adults. This includes TV shows, movies, music, books, magazines, and the like.

For that reason, we have set *very* strict filtering limits for our family, by refusing to watch, read, or support any form of entertainment that includes promiscuity, dark magic of any sort, taking the Lord's name in vain, or glorification of anything that would not be pleasing to the Lord. While this conviction stems from our faith in Jesus Christ, we also see that heavily filtering our entertainment removes temptations and allowances that could alter the success of our marriage and family.

Let me explain our entertainment filters a little further.

We believe very strongly in not supporting any form of entertainment that promotes *promiscuity* in any way; and for us, promiscuity is a broad category that includes lots of little specifics, such as immodestly dressed characters, for example.

There are a few reasons why we won't be entertained by even small amounts of promiscuity. Many men claim to be faithful husbands to their wives, but find no harm in lustfully ogling over a scantily clad woman in a movie. Just the same, many wives claim faithfulness in their marriage, but find nothing more enjoyable than being curled up on the sofa reading the latest romance novel, filled with explicit adjectives used to excite the imagination and build unrealistic expectations. With spouses exposing themselves to that kind of entertainment, it doesn't take long for each one to find fault in the other, as they just aren't measuring up to what they are 'supposed to be'. The world wants us to think that these forms of entertainment really don't affect us, but if we honestly examine them, we can easily see the damage that is done.

Promiscuity in entertainment also damages the perspective and expectations of children, specifically in teens and young adults, giving them unrealistic ideas of what their future relationships should look like. And while young children may not face the same fleshly temptations as teens/adults, exposure to promiscuity in their entertainment lays a damaging foundation for them as they age.

We know that there are occasions where promiscuity will try to creep in our choice of entertainment - for instance, scantily clad dancers shown quickly during a football game. We've learned to just rely on the Holy Spirit in these cases, and to be very transparent with our kids, as the Lord leads in each situation. If we need to turn off the TV, we will. Simple as that.

Our family has also chosen to filter out all types of *dark magic and sorcery* from our entertainment choices, and at times, we even include 'harmless magic' in that filter. I'll touch on harmless magic first. We are somewhat sporadic with this, trying to remain sensitive to the Lord's direction in any given circumstance. While we might be ok with an educational, personified cartoon such as 'The Magic School Bus' (affectionately referred to in our house as 'The *Science* School Bus'), we might steer clear of other magical entertainment, and here's why: While we believe in encouraging our children's imagination, we see a big difference in personification and using a wand or a crystal ball for results. Although many people don't see the harm in this, we recognize that exposing children to magic indirectly teaches them not to live in reality, but in fantasy. We also believe it teaches them to look for help in places other than Jesus. This doesn't mean you won't ever catch us watching Frosty the Snowman or Cinderella, but it does mean that we are careful not to expose our kids to too much fantasy - again, at the direction of the Holy Spirit.

In the cases of dark magic and sorcery, though, there are no exceptions. That's simply because of our belief in what the Bible says about magic and sorcery.

Honoring the name of the Lord, too, is a very important entertainment filter to us, as we believe He created us and sacrificed Himself to save us from our sins. For that reason, along with our support of the Third Commandment, we have decided not to support any kind of entertainment that misuses His name in any way. Should we be watching, listening to, or reading any form of entertainment that takes His name in vain, we will stop. If others are present, it even gives us an opportunity for sharing our decision to honor His name above all else.

With this said, we do believe that historical documentaries, especially live footage, that may take the Lord's name in vain are a little different, as they may not qualify as entertainment, and so we exercise more grace at the direction of the Holy Spirit in these situations.

The final filter of entertainment we mentioned is *glorification of anything that would not be pleasing to the Lord*; and we left that category a little broad on purpose. Basically, this filter includes anything else that we would discern as Biblically inappropriate.

While we are extremely cautious on what entertainment we expose ourselves and our family to, we don't, however, want to disregard *all* movies that have certain negative content; as long as that negative content is ultimately used to build a story that glorifies Jesus. For instance drinking, drugs, or violence are all negative content - but if those examples are included in ways that can show Christ's victory over sin, we *want* to support that particular entertainment.

Some movies, books, or songs have very inspirational messages and positive elements of overcoming struggles and sins, and we believe that as long as those negative situations are used in a story that ultimately glorifies God, they are alright. (We do believe there are some exceptions here - for instance, scantily clad characters or physically intimate scenes, are *never* acceptable, even if they are part of story of overcoming struggle. That's because those particular examples will *never* bring God glory, as they are so tempting in nature to see or read about).

The point is, we don't just blindly head into entertainment, because once you've been exposed to these things, the damage has already been done. This is especially true in visual exposure, as images can stay in your mind for a lifetime.

For that reason, we make conscious efforts to avoid accidentally stumbling on entertainment that goes against our convictions listed here. We do that in a few ways, one of which being: we research what we can on PluggedIn.com, a Christian entertainment review site that highlights positive and negative elements in movies, shows, songs, books, etc. These reviews give us a very good idea of what to expect from entertainment in the way of violence, crude language, spiritual content, and more.

Another way we avoid potentially negative material is by not watching commercials during a TV show or sports broadcast. Commercials increasingly present more and more inappropriate material and temptations that are not Biblical at all. Some ads we would deem as blatantly inappropriate, such as a beer commercial boasting a near naked girl swimming in the ocean while drinking from a colorful can; while others are more subtly inappropriate, such as a car commercial that excites a covetous nature. Both examples, though, encourage ungodly behavior, as they directly contradict the Ten Commandments. Therefore, we choose to not expose our family to them at all. We simply pause them or turn them off.

We are aware of parental control settings, and controlled streaming devices, such as ClearPlay; however, we choose not to use these services for filtering purposes. We believe that if certain parts of entertainment need to be deleted or adjusted, then we shouldn't be supporting it in the first place. Watching the latest Hollywood movie on ClearPlay, for instance, may shield our family from certain inappropriate material, but knowing that we watched that movie could mislead someone else who was unaware of our decision to censor. We just believe it's best to stick with the entertainment choices that need no adjusting.

TWELVE

Dressing Modestly

I like cute clothes and the latest trends (well some of them!) just as much as the next girl out there, but I have found that all too often cute clothes and trendy styles reveal everything *but* God's glory. So, with that in mind, my husband and I have set some standards in the way that we dress to ensure that we don't cause someone else to fall into the very temptations we have been convicted to avoid! This generally affects *my* wardrobe instead of his (bummer!).

The fact of the matter, though, is that styles that accentuate a woman's figure in different ways can be tempting to a man. Like it or not, low cut shirts, mini-skirts, and midriff baring tops draw attention to our bodies and tempt men with inappropriate thoughts.

I'll admit, this conviction was a tough issue for me. In fact, I resisted following through with this conviction for awhile. I came up with every excuse I could think of too, but ultimately, I decided to quit ignoring the constant reminding of the Holy Spirit.

As a result, my attitude of "I can't help what he thinks" slowly shifted to "Actually, I *can* help what he thinks - by not wearing clothing that would provoke inappropriate thoughts". That mindset ultimately convinced me to begin to dress more modestly.

I'm no longer willing to wear certain things in public and possibly tempt someone else by leaving such little room for the imagination.

Disclaimer here - please don't misunderstand me and think that I have the deluded idea that I have a super model body. Let's be real - I've had four children. But perfect hourglass figures aren't the only thing that can be tempting to the opposite sex. All women of all different shapes and sizes can tempt a man with inappropriate thoughts.

So... where do I draw the line? What do I (we) consider as inappropriate dress for our family?

Simply put: anything that reveals or accentuates a woman's body, specifically her chest or backside. We recognize these specifics as the main 'problem areas' for men, and so clothing that reveals or accentuates them can very understandably tempt a man with sinful thoughts.

Our solution to that problem is for the girls in our family to cover up our bodies with clothing that doesn't call attention to those particular areas. It means that perhaps we wear a scarf with a lower cut top. Or we wear a tunic style top when wearing more form fitted pants, like leggings. It means we wear a longer style of boyfriend shorts as opposed to daisy dukes. We trade halter tops for tanks with more coverage, and string bikinis for tankinis or one pieces.

It's not easy, and can be frustrating, but we are committed to dressing modestly.

We can't control what others wear, but we *can* control what we wear; so my girls will learn by my example what a woman should and shouldn't wear in order to bring God glory.

I mentioned that this was a difficult conviction to convince myself to follow through with in the first place, and it was; but once I finally decided to surrender, I made the mistake of going all in... and then some. I took off on my race for modesty without a second thought, which proved to be incredibly frustrating for me because, while I'd surrendered to God in the conviction to dress modestly, I'd completely forgotten to be sensitive to the personal direction of the Holy Spirit as to what was considered appropriate and what was not. Without meaning to, I used up all of my energy at the beginning of the race, and found myself burnt out a mile in.

Here's what happened: I knew that I was convicted to dress modestly, and so I hastily concluded that the only way that I could bring God glory, and my husband honor, was by only wearing modest *dresses*! So, I took my good intentions to the local consignment shop and racked up on adorable dresses!

This actually got me excited (funny how new clothes can do that!) about my newfound conviction, and, for a little while, all seemed right in the world. I loved being dressed up in the mornings, holding my little ones at the door as we waved Daddy off to work. It made me feel successful as a housewife. I can actually remember thinking *"How many other stay-at-home moms spend their days in dresses, ha! Probably not very many!"*

It took me about a week to find out why.

Sure, standing at the door feeling a sense of pride in my appearance was nice, but spending the following 12 hours in a dress became less and less exciting each day.

Picking up food underneath the table, chasing a toddler around, making the beds, and being spit up on, along with conquering all of my other daily chores at home became more and more frustrating than they ever had been before - not just because I was in a dress *that* day, but because I had bound myself to a dress for eternity! Never again would I run down the hall playing hide-and-seek in blue jeans and a T-shirt! Never again would I rake leaves in the yard in my yoga pants (which... by the way I don't do yoga, I just love the pants...), and never again would I just have a lazy PJ day! My initial excitement of a few cute dresses had quickly turned into a resentful compulsion that exhausted and frustrated me. I felt like a failure. They say pride goeth before the fall... and it does! And great was my fall!

After a few days of trying to shake off the failure feelings with no avail, I went to my husband and unloaded. I explained that while I wanted to dress modestly to glorify God, this wearing a dress every day was a *huge* ball and chain.

The simple fact that I was even telling him all of this made me feel like an even bigger failure! I wanted to say to myself 'oh come on now and just wear a dress, girl, and get over it!' And I think I almost expected him to say that same sort of thing... just maybe a little more gently; But to my surprise, he didn't. In fact, he suggested I *stop* wearing dresses every day! Whew!! What a relief.

He went on to explain that while he had been initially supportive of my goal, his main concern for me and our daughters was the conviction of modesty, not my goal of wearing dresses. He said that he felt as though I could still meet the high standard of modesty we want to set for our family in other, less restrictive ways, and so suggested that I relax my rules and just focus on fully covering the problem areas that men struggle with. So, I went back to square one and started over, and with his direction managed to come up with a basic standard of modesty for myself and our daughters for when we're out in public that is effective, yet not overwhelming.

I no doubt had good intentions with my initial goal of wearing dresses all the time, but my failure to prayerfully consider exactly how to follow through with my conviction left me wanting to just give up altogether. Thankfully, though, the adjustments I made worked well for us, and are the same standards we will teach our children to set for themselves one day (keeping in mind that they may alter these standards as adults, according to the direction of the Holy Spirit in their own lives).

It's important for us all to remember that while our standards of dress may be different than yours, that doesn't necessarily make them legalistically right or wrong.

We believe that Christians have a Biblical responsibility to dress modestly, but that each family should decide for themselves what that standard of modesty should be, through the direction of the Holy Spirit (are you tired of me saying this yet? Seeing a trend?!). We know that God can (and does!) direct different families in different ways on the same issue - all for His glory!

While we *can* say without a doubt that *certain* styles of dress will *never* bring glory to God, we *can't* say that *our* style of dress is the *only* one that will.

THIRTEEN

Home Schooling

Our conviction to homeschool goes hand in hand with us deciding for me to be a stay-at-home mom; it just takes it to the next level. As you know, we believe that the Lord blessed us with children that He wants us to raise at home; but we also believe that raising them doesn't stop when they reach kindergarten age - it continues - and *we* believe it should continue *at home*. This particular conviction directly results from our past, specifically my past.

As I've shared, I grew up in a very strict Christian home. I did, however, attend public school grades K-12.

While boundaries and rules were set by my parents at home, boundaries and rules were challenged by my peers away from home. Kids who were raised differently than I was didn't understand the rules and regulations that my parents had set for me, and as a result, I found myself the brunt of many jokes.

Unfortunately, as I got older, I ultimately decided that I would rather fit in with my friends and have what seemed like harmless fun with them, than listen to what my parents said. As you can imagine, this caused some frustration at home; in fact, my parents will not hesitate to tell you that I was a complete nightmare to live with at 14 years old! I won't tell you the feeling was mutual (...wait...oops!).

What I realize in retrospect, though, is that it was around age 14 that I began struggling internally, and unfortunately, I began lashing out at my parents because of it. I'd been taught right and wrong by them, according to God's standards, my entire life, but the outside world was battling for my soul.

That internal struggle led me to begin desperately trying to reason with my parents, so that I could have my cake and eat it too. I wanted to please them and please my friends. I wanted to fit in, but not disappoint.

I realized pretty quickly, though, that my parents were set in their ways, and they weren't changing; so, eventually, I quit trying to change their minds, and just started lying. I quit asking permission for things I knew they wouldn't approve of, and just started asking permission for the things I knew they would. Once I received their approval, I used the freedom they had given me to just do what I wanted to do in the first place behind their backs. And in my mind, it worked. My relationship with my parents got better, I finally fit in with my friends, and I believed in a God who would forgive me. Perfect world.

Except I also see, in retrospect, that I was on the road to Hell.

Everything my parents had worked so hard to teach me about God, I tossed out the window in order to fit in with my peers. At that pivotal age of 14, without truly realizing *or* caring, I threw it all away for fleeting fun. Thankfully, the fun I had as a naive 14 year old didn't come with serious consequences, but it was sin nonetheless.

A few years later, I moved out of my parents house at age 18, and into an apartment with two close girl friends. We made memories there that I wouldn't trade, and memories there that now shame me to even think about.

Worst of all, my habit of lying continued, and grew. And all the while, even though I no longer lived at home, I maintained the two separate lives that I had mastered years earlier: the one my parents wanted me to live, and the one I actually lived. This makes it sound like my parents were completely naive to my decisions, which would be doing them a disservice to suggest. Though I surely fooled them some, they were also probably a lot more aware of my double life than I would like to admit. But they prayed me through it, and their love and guidance along the way has ultimately helped shape many of our convictions. Anyway, my parents weren't dumb. I was!

This double life was a vicious cycle, though, and continued for awhile... how long exactly, I don't know.

Somewhere along the way, I began dating - which proved to cause an immense amount of heartache, since my priorities weren't in order; but through God's grace alone, I got through it, and ended up married to my husband. And it wasn't long before we both realized that living for the God I said I believed in, instead of for *ourselves*, was the only way that we would ever be successful in our marriage, or in our future family.

Accepting and surrendering to Jesus as our Savior was the best decision we ever made, and it allowed the Lord to use our past to shape our future, and the future of our family.

Looking back at my life, I realize that I wouldn't have experienced the struggles that I did had I been homeschooled. No, it wouldn't have ensured that I'd *never* make a mistake, but it absolutely would have lessened the chances of the rebellion encouraged by the friends I made at school.

I am also eternally thankful that God is sovereign and can work anything He chooses for good, because in His sovereignty, He chose not to reveal the need to homeschool to my parents (because they definitely would have done it if He had!); and through that, He worked for good what satan intended for evil. I met many wonderful people in school, made many lasting friendships, and even met my husband!

Good friendships aside, though, I was led astray in the public school system, and was on the road to Hell - something I'm not willing to chance for my children.

It was critical for us to recognize that the majority of the poor decisions I made in my teenage/young adult years (some that could have cost me my life), and most of the heartache I experienced was a direct result of my being inappropriately influenced by outside peers.

Please understand, this is not me shirking responsibility for my sinful actions. The blame doesn't rest at the feet of my parents, nor does it rest at the feet of the friends I made. The fault is mine alone. *I* messed up because *I* chose to give into bad influences.

The point is, had those bad influences not been present in my life in the first place, I wouldn't have had the same temptations to give into them. With that knowledge, my husband and I agree that the probable risks of going to public school far outweigh the potential benefits, and so have therefore decided to homeschool our children.

Oh, I've heard every argument against homeschooling, but I'll save you the time and tell you that we disagree with all of them.

As the Lord allows, we are committed to following through with our conviction to homeschool our kids, all the way through high school, and are committed to preparing them for the real world, through a Biblical lens. They will get a proper education without the outside pressure of peers who have been raised differently, and by the time they graduate high school, we are praying that they will be strong enough in their own convictions to live lives that are pleasing to God outside of our home.

Does that mean that we stay inside all the time, never stepping foot into the real world? No! We are called to be *in* the world while not *of* it.

Will our kids be allowed to have friends? Of course they will - like minded friends that we approve of.

Will they get jobs? Yes.
Even the girls? As single young adults, under our authority, yes. It will be up to them and the direction of the Holy Spirit, as well as their potential future husbands as to whether or not they work outside the home once they leave the nest.

See, our goal is to teach our children how to live in the world as a light for Christ, rather than the world teaching them how to live in darkness. Simply put, that takes time.

We've heard of other Christian families who have chosen to put their children in public schools for the sole purpose of being the light to a lost world, but we strongly believe (and have seen first hand through my life) that a child's mind is too pliable to risk the potential danger that is almost certain to come from the very ones they're attempting to shine to.

Consider this example: You don't send a new recruit into battle without proper training, even if there's a need for another warrior. Sending them out too early would likely have a devastating effect.

It's our belief that our children *are* those new recruits, for Christ, and that their proper training will take about 18 years, give or take a year or two. We can't, and we won't, risk the devastation of sending them out into the world too early.

We believe that pressure from peers is the *most* damaging aspect of public, and even private schools, but curriculum is another reason we have chosen to homeschool.

Public school curriculum is governmentally regulated curriculum, and it blatantly goes against Biblical doctrine. Not only are children in public schools learning and embracing doctrines like the Big Bang Theory and the Theory of Evolution, but Christ has been completely removed, and expression of the Christian faith is increasingly discouraged and prohibited.

So why would I, as a devout Christian parent, send my precious gift from God to a place that discourages Him, and teaches a completely different theology? It doesn't make sense.

Furthermore, we understand the Bible to prohibit Christians from giving children an education contrary to a Biblical worldview. Homeschooling may not be the way for everyone, but learning from a Biblical worldview is, and that's just not happening in public schools (or in many private schools too). It's frustrating that, to give kids an education from a Biblical worldview in this day in age, requires some financial sacrifice; but frustrating or not, it's a decision that we wholeheartedly believe is worth the sacrifices.

School shootings, bullying, gangs, and other forms of violence are also reasons to consider homeschooling, though in our opinion, are actually the least worrisome.

Now let me take a moment to clarify here: We recognize that God places us in certain situations, and He places teachers (*especially*) in schools to show the love of Jesus to others.

I have many friends who have taught, or who are currently teaching, in schools today, and I love them very much. Even my sister, who shares many of the same convictions we do, is currently a teacher. Teachers and other staff members can make a positive difference in the lives of others, and we fully believe that God can and will call certain men and women to teach in both public and private school settings, for His glory; and we encourage and support those teachers as they head into battle daily.

It's unfortunate that the truth God has led us to share about our view of current public education will likely offend many people (not my goal!), but we also believe it's a truth that is overlooked more often than not, and one our family is very passionate about.

Of course, there will always be exceptions that really do prevent families from being able to afford a Biblical worldview education for their children, but like in so many other cases, we believe these true exceptional cases are few and far between. The majority of the time, 'unaffordability' or 'unavailability' usually just boils down to parents being *unwilling* to sacrifice.

For those few cases, though, that truly *do* prevent parents from homeschooling, or sending their children to a private Christian school for that Biblical worldview, we believe that meeting that need is a responsibility of the church; and we would encourage the body of Christ to come together in discernment, generosity, and love, in order to protect the minds of the children involved, as God leads in each situation.

And, in case you're wondering, we have no desire to be the judge of those who choose to send their children to public schools, so rest easy if you do... I'm not looking to condemn you in this book. That's between you and God, not you and me!

[As sure as I say that, though, I'll still be accused of judging others for making personal decisions contrary to mine, but that's ok. One thing I have learned over time, is that living a Christian life requires not only sacrifice, but suffering; and if our family has to suffer persecutions because we have chosen to speak the truth as God has led us to, so be it. I would never say these things to the world if God didn't impress it upon my heart to do so, but He has, and so I will].

I just ask that, when you find yourself offended and angry at my beliefs, you remember that I have prayerfully considered every word I have written, and fully believe God wants me to speak them, in total transparency and love, for the purpose of His Kingdom.

We do understand and respect that ultimately each family has to choose for themselves what education is appropriate and what is not, but we also believe that if more families truly listened to God and sought His direction in how to educate their children, they would agree that education from a Biblical worldview via homeschool is the best option.

FOURTEEN

Careful Choice of Friends

I shared in our conviction about homeschooling that we feel very strongly about not exposing our children to the outside pressures of peers who aren't raised in the same ways they are.

This not only includes peers that our children would be exposed to in a public school arena, but also includes peers that they would be exposed to in other places, even including church.

This conviction, too, is a direct result of our reflection on my past.

I was raised in a strict Christian home, remember? We *never* missed a Sunday. Or a Wednesday night for that matter. In fact, if there was an event of any kind at church, we were there.

So it's no surprise that I attended our youth group.

Now, I'll pick on churches for a minute. One would think that a church youth group is a perfectly harmless place. After all, it's a place that most parents would happily encourage their teenager to attend.

It is my experience though, that unfortunate as it may be, many church youth groups contain the same kinds of pressures that public school systems do. While there are *some* youth leaders that keep a tight rein on the activity going on inside their church, many church youth groups fail to encourage teens to honor God through behavior, dress, conversation, etc; but instead, encourage a broad spectrum of corrupt behavior through tolerance and poor leadership (please understand, I am not singling out our church or any specific church - our church's youth leader is amazing! I'm just speaking generally here).

But these are church kids, you say. They're *surely* going to be more of a positive influence, right? Not necessarily.
While most of the kids in a youth group do attend church, usually most of them attend public school as well, and consequently interact with peers that are not raised with the same values that they are. You remember what a mess that was for me.
Furthermore, not all church going families have Biblical values.
I've already touched on how worldly pressures from peers at school (both public *and* private) can negatively influence children, even those with a strong Christian upbringing; so it's no surprise that these negative influences trickle into church youth groups through teens who have been influenced outside of them.
Now, throw in the aspects of raging teenage hormones, the strong desire to fit in, and the normal awkwardness that the teenage years bring anyway, and you end up with a disaster: seemingly trustworthy kids who are learning about God's word during Bible study, and living like they've never heard it in the fellowship time immediately following.
I wish I could say differently, but my youth group as a teen was no exception to this. In fact, I specifically remember playing hide and seek one night at a poorly monitored co-ed youth group lock in (hey, there's a great idea, NOT!) and walking in on a hook up. And these were two kids who were at church every time the doors opened too!

Considering all of *that*, my husband and I *refuse* to make change after change after change to our family's lives for the benefit of our children, just to be done in at church!
Do we think all youth groups and youth leaders are evil? No, of course not. We believe that God has called and placed people in youth leadership positions at churches - including ours - for a reason, ultimately being so that He may be glorified! The reality of it is that many teens will have

no exposure to Christ other than that of a church youth group! We realize, though, that as parents, we have a responsibility to use extreme discernment in every situation involving our children's peers, including those at church.

The bottom line for *us*, is that the chance of negative peer pressure at church is still too great to risk if left unmonitored. And while I've been harping on potential negative peer pressure at church, that goes for anywhere - the soccer field, the dance studio, the playground - you get it.

We don't want to just hope that our kids make good friends, we want to be intentional in guiding them to.
For that reason, we will prayerfully consider who we allow our children to form strong friendships with, and we will monitor their influence on our family first hand, even in church settings.
No, we can't be in every situation with every child of ours all the time (we are outnumbered with four kids!); but we can make sure that if *we* are unable to personally monitor our children at church, that there is a trustworthy person that we have a personal relationship with in place to monitor them - especially in a youth setting.

With regard to strong friendships made through any outlet, we will make a point to know and trust the parents of that peer, and we will often suggest our home as the place for our kids to fellowship. Outside venues and the homes of friends will not necessarily be off limits, but will be strongly considered - to *ensure* that our children will not be exposed to the very things we work to shield them from.
We imagine, though, that most of our kids' friends will have like minded parents with whom we will have built a relationship, and so fellowship at their homes will likely not be an issue.

While we want to closely monitor the friendships that our children make, so that they are not led astray, we also want to be intentional in teaching them how to be friendly with everyone they come in contact with. They don't have to be best buddies with everyone in order to be friendly to them!
We want to involve our kids in certain activities with the world, that we are able to closely monitor, so as to show them through total transparency

just how badly the world needs Jesus. This is how we believe using your children to 'be the light' should happen. In order to train them effectively to be mighty warriors for Christ, we are going to have to expose them to the world along the way; otherwise they will be completely unprepared for real life when they're adults. The difference is, though, that we are exposing them to the world while modeling the example right in front of them, walking alongside them every step of the way, directing them, correcting them, and encouraging them to live for Jesus in each different situation. For instance, our oldest son started playing soccer at a local complex as a 4 year old, and because we have been fully present at every practice and every game, we've been able to not only talk about the behavior he's witnessed from his teammates (both good and bad), but we've been able to show him how to intentionally share the love of Jesus with others in different ways. One way we've done this is by working together with our kids at home during the week preparing little gifts for the team that somehow points them to the gospel. We want our children to learn how to choose close friends wisely, as well as to learn how to be friendly and loving towards everyone, even those who misbehave, or do things differently than we do. The key to this, though, is that we (or someone we trust) will always be present during their involvement in activities such as these, in order to encourage positive friendships.

Many people have scoffed at our decision to intentionally monitor our children's friendships in these ways, and have specifically accused me of being a 'helicopter mom', and hey, that's ok. I know I can't please everyone, and honestly, I'm not looking to. I'm looking to please just One; and I believe that He has led us to set these boundaries, and share them with you!
Despite what people think, we look forward to many strong and lasting friendships that our children will enjoy!

Along with closely monitoring our *children's* choice of friends, we monitor *ours* as well. This, unfortunately, can be a hairy topic, but a necessary one for us as Christians.
Friends, by definition, are special people in our lives with whom we spend time. It's those people who we talk to on a regular basis, and who - intentionally or not - influence us.

Many parents warn their kids to 'make good friends' because they know that the people their kids spend time with will influence them, either for good or bad (unfortunately, they stop at the *warning* and don't find ways to prevent this from happening - but we've already covered that!).

As it turns out, the same applies for adults.

Our friends will influence *us, too* - for good or bad. So a careful choice of friends for us, as adults, is important too.

Does that mean we never associate with people who believe differently than we do, or take part in things that we do not? No! Not at all.

As Christians, we don't believe that we are *better* than others, but we do believe that we are *sanctified*, or set apart. That means that there is a visible difference between the lives we lead and the lives of those who don't believe the same things that we do. Being *set apart* from the world gives Christians a different lens with which to see others through. Looking through this lens helps us determine who we should form friendships with, and why.

Christians are supposed to be loving and friendly to everyone, yes. But we're also supposed to carefully discern who our *friends* should be, to ensure that we surround ourselves with good influences, and are able to intentionally and effectively witness to those who are lost. Sure, only God truly knows each person's heart - but we have a responsibility to observe someone's fruit to the best of our abilities, which helps us make the right choices in friendships.

Unfortunately, to observe others' fruit often gives Christians a bad rap, and so many believers shy away from it, in fear of offending someone; and in turn, they begin making allowances for sin. The result is a bunch of watered down believers who are unable to confidently lead anyone to Christ. We want to be different.

We are aware that many people will try to twist around this particular conviction, for one reason or another, and we have unfortunately found ourselves in extremely frustrating positions before, due to just that.

We just try to remember that while Jesus ate with sinners, He used it as an opportunity to show His love to them, not to participate in their sin or simply enjoy their company. We also recall when Jesus gave Christians the Great Commission - He called us to make *disciples* of all nations, not *friends* of all nations.

Friends are great, and we are blessed to have many wonderful friends, and look forward to making many more. At the same time, we feel extremely blessed to be able to witness to others who do not share our values, through appropriate and friendly fellowship.

The bottom line is that we believe that God has placed all of the people He has in our family's lives for a reason, and we're committed to bringing Him glory through *our* choice of friendships and *our* children's.

FIFTEEN

Sobriety in Alcohol, Tobacco, and Other Recreational Drugs

This chapter is no doubt the shortest chapter in this book, as this particular conviction doesn't require a lot of explanation.

Most parents would agree that at least some form of monitoring the use of alcohol, tobacco, and recreational drugs is appropriate.

We all know that any of these activities can lead to trouble.

So, as to ensure that we avoid that trouble for ourselves, *and* in an effort to avoid confusion for others, we have decided to maintain total sobriety in each of these areas.

SIXTEEN

Selective Support of Businesses and Corporations

The Bible is very specific when it comes to instructing Christians not to participate in, or even *tolerate* certain activities, so we have set a standard for our family to ensure that to the best of our knowledge and ability, and as God leads, we will refrain from financially supporting certain companies who blatantly disrespect the Word of God through their hearty approval of sinful behaviors.

While it's not always an easy one, it's a pretty simple conviction: don't spend money at certain places.

Now, we believe that God can and will call people - even us - to places that abuse His Word, for the sake of furthering His Kingdom, but that doesn't mean we tolerate sin by financially supporting those businesses. There have actually been multiple instances where friends or family have asked us to join them and even offered to treat us at a business we don't support, and we've accepted. Likewise, we've been given gift cards to businesses we don't support, and found ourselves wandering the aisles of stores we otherwise wouldn't. On the surface, it might seem like in those cases we were supporting businesses we'd been convicted not to support, but in reality, that would not be the case. Yet again, we have learned to see others through eyes of grace, having found ourselves in situations that appeared hypocritical when in reality, they were not.

In the same vein, though, our convictions can provide us an opportunity to be honest about where God has led us and why. Perhaps a friend invites us to a restaurant that we have chosen not to support. While we certainly wouldn't want to come across self righteous in our decision not to support a business they liked, our suggestion to meet elsewhere because of our conviction may have greater, more positive effects than we think. Maybe that friend begins to ponder what he's financially willing to support, or perhaps he's just encouraged in his faith to see someone truly standing up for something they believe in.

Of course, I know first hand that there are people who would truly take offense at our refusal to support a business they support, and persecute us for our choice. But that's certainly not a reason not to have standards. Furthermore, the Bible tells us to rejoice in persecution!

Here's the bottom line. The decisions we make about who to do business with and who not to are careful decisions that we believe God has led us to make, and we aim to be true to this conviction regardless of what others may think. And while we're not always immediately aware of every business's acceptance or promotion of sin, we know that eventually, everything that is hidden will be brought into the light, according to the Word of God. And as we're made aware, we will stand for Jesus.

There are plenty of ways that a company can disrespect God and His Word, of course, but sexual immorality (specifically in the forms of indecency and physical provocativeness) and homosexuality are two specific sins that we've noticed are becoming more and more widely encouraged, accepted, and most importantly promoted by businesses for financial gain.

We understand that every single company out there will have *someone* in it who supports something that we don't agree with; *but,* we see a big difference in a *person* disrespecting God's Word through their own support of sin, as opposed to a *company* corporately, publicly, and unapologetically supporting - and worse, encouraging that sin.

All this considered, we have decided for ourselves that, as the Spirit leads, we will not directly financially support a company that publicly encourages sins that we are forbidden to tolerate as Christians.
On the flip side, we have every desire *to* financially support companies that publicly take a stand against sins, and encourage people in their Christian faith. We believe these companies have chosen to use their business as a platform for Jesus, and want to give them our business as much as we are able. That's why we are happy to make every effort to do business with places like Chick-Fil-A, Jim Bob's, and Hobby Lobby.

Unfortunately, we anticipate as time goes on, more and more companies will become more and more outspoken on their acceptance and support of sinful behaviors, and we recognize that all of this is really just the fulfilling of prophecy. The book of Revelation reveals to us that there will come a time where people will have to choose between buying or selling food and standing up for their faith by refusing to accept the mark of the beast. In those days, there are no exceptions. People will literally starve for their refusal to support sin. This is just the beginning.
We remain encouraged, though, that God will reward our daily choices to deny our flesh and live by the Spirit!

A few final thoughts on this issue that I believe are worth mentioning are as follows:
While we take Ephesians 5:11 seriously with regard to 'exposing the evil deeds of darkness', we don't believe that necessarily means we stand on the street corner with a list of names of companies we refuse to support. We want to be loving, not hateful, in our approach of exposing, as we believe you can 'attract more flies with honey than vinegar'. We want to expose these companies through relevant conversation, or simply through our action of not making a purchase when it would seem appropriate - not through phone calls or Facebook posts each week with the names of the latest additions to our 'bad list'. Not to mention, that sets us up to look

like hypocrites, should God lead us to one of those places, even if we never spend a cent with them!

Bottom line - we try to be sensitive to the Holy Spirit's direction, and you should too! He will guide us to courageously stand up for our conviction at the appropriate time in the appropriate way.

SEVENTEEN

No Santa Claus, No Easter Bunny, No Tooth Fairy

Just when you thought we couldn't get any crazier, we go and take crazy to a whole new level!

Ok... let's start with Santa.
We have decided that it is best for *our* family to not celebrate 'Santa Claus'.

While we don't believe that Santa is harmful as a make believe character, we do believe that telling our children that he's real could be, for a few reasons.
Now, both my husband and I grew up believing in Santa Claus, and upon finding out the truth, each understood it as a fun little game that our parents chose to play with us and nothing more.
But it isn't always as cut and dry as that.

A friend once shared with me her story about finding out that Santa Claus was not real. She, too, grew up in a strong Christian home, and always attended church with her family. Instead of chalking up Santa to a fun little game, though, when *she* found out that he wasn't real, she began questioning the reality of Jesus too. She explained to me that she associated both Santa and Jesus with happy, joyful, Christmas characters. All of her life, she'd learned that they *both* wanted you to be good, *both* always saw your actions, and *both* made you very happy. The only problem now though, was that she'd just found out that her parents had been making one of them up all of these years, so naturally, doubt and confusion set in. She went to her mom with the simple question: "Mom, if Santa's not real, does that mean Jesus is not real either?".

Now, I don't expect *all* children to have that response; as I said, neither my husband nor I did. But the fact that it's a possibility is enough for us.

Furthermore, I would hate to spend all the time and energy we are spending raising our children in the direction of the Lord, just to risk them questioning everything because of a funny little make believe character.

One other reason we don't care for celebrating Santa is that it encourages reward for good works. While good works are important, Jesus taught that *faith* is what matters, and through that faith will come works, which we may never get rewarded for here on Earth.

As for the Easter Bunny and the Tooth Fairy, the same things apply - we don't want to risk confusing our kids for a little bit of fun.
Our kids will still get money when they lose a tooth, they will still enjoy Easter candy, and we'll still swap gifts at Christmas. But, they will know up front Who's real, and who's make believe.

We've also had a few people question how we plan to keep our children from spoiling the fun of others who do celebrate these characters. Here's our answer: While we can't promise that their innocent responses wouldn't spoil a surprise, we will encourage them to redirect these potential conversations to Jesus.
For instance, when someone asks them: "What did Santa bring you, sweetie?', we will teach them to respond with something like this: "I don't know about that, but *Jesus* gave me a gift! He died on the cross for me!".

We may not believe in celebrating these characters in our family, but our intent is certainly not for our children to spoil the fun of others; and so we will continue to raise our children to respect the decisions of other families, even if they disagree, the same way we hope to be respected for ours.

EIGHTEEN

Not Celebrating Halloween

Another holiday tradition we felt led to discard was the celebration of Halloween. Again, both my husband and I dressed up and trick-or-treated every Halloween, and are no worse for the wear from doing so, at least I don't think we are! We just felt God leading us to do otherwise for our family after we attended a church service that highlighted the history of Halloween. After doing some more research on our own, we decided that it was not a holiday that honored God *at all*.

The basics of what we learned boil down to this: the traditions of Halloween originated over 2,000 years ago, from the Celtic's belief that, for one day, the living world could coexist with the dead in different ways. While some drew comfort from communication with their deceased loved ones (which is unbiblical), most people spent that day in fear of demonic spirits. As to ward off these spirits, the Celt's concocted different means of protection that morphed into the very icons we know and love today, such as the jack-o-lantern, dressing in costume, and the very act of 'trick or treating'. I'll spare you the *full* details of Halloween history (though I do encourage you to look it up yourself), and leave it at that, but from that alone, you can see how these traditions fail to honor God.

That's why we decided that our family is better off not celebrating it.

NINETEEN

Preparing Our Children for Courtship

Ahhhh, dating.

For many adults, myself included, the memory of dating brings to mind a twinge of excitement... followed closely by an embarrassing amount of head scratching, wondering why we ever put ourselves through some of the things we did.

So much fun, and yet so much heartache.

Well, what if you, as a parent, could eliminate the heartache from your children's lives, and just leave them with the fun? The joy. The bliss. The positive.

How do you do that, you ask?

We believe the answer is to rule out *dating* and, instead, prepare them to *court*.

Courting is different from dating, because it gives a different purpose to the relationship - one that puts specific focus and strong emphasis on the future. Dating tends to focus more on the present, while placing the future of the relationship in a hopeful state of fantasy.

We want our kids to focus on the *future* benefits of a potential relationship before focusing on the *present* ones. If the future relationship shows instability, a present relationship isn't worth investing in, as it will certainly lead to heartache!

Now - we are a few years away from our kids even *noticing* the opposite sex yet, but our plan is to keep them focused on serving Jesus once they do reach those years as a youth, in order to avoid them wasting their precious time and energy on a boyfriend or girlfriend who lacks the future potential of a godly spouse. Furthermore, we know that God will honor this commitment by bringing our children the right person in His timing.

We have experienced first hand the frustrations, temptations, and heartaches from dating, and we realize now that it's because we had the wrong *purpose*.
It happens all the time.
He likes her because she's pretty, or she likes him because he's popular. She wants a boyfriend because all her friends have one, or he wants a girlfriend so that he can have some fun. People pair up in meaningless relationships all the time without ever considering the future damage that can come from insecurity, popularity, or promiscuity.

We also realize that even in relationships that show serious potential, there are physical temptations that are beyond dangerous when not controlled. So, along with teaching our kids how to focus on the future benefits of a potential relationship, we also want to provide them with the safety net of accountability once they begin a courtship. We will let the Lord guide us on the specifics of that once the time comes, but we will likely implement some sort of chaperoning system.
And, because we believe that women were created more emotional than men, we will *all* rely on their father's objective guidance to ensure that they will successfully find *true* love!

TWENTY

Family Worship

The last of our convictions that I am sharing with you is our decision to worship together in church as an entire family. This decision, too, stems from the conviction of raising our children *ourselves*, as opposed to sending them out into the care of others on a regular basis.

Gathering together *as a family* in church is important to us for a few reasons.

One important reason we choose to do this is to protect our children from potential negative influences of other children or youth when we are not around - it's the same things I mentioned before in previous chapters. Now before you get all upset that we are suggesting the members of our church have kids or youth that are bad influences, let me stop you; I never said that. In fact, on the contrary, I am very encouraged in seeing so many families at our church raising their children to fear the Lord and shine for Him. We just don't want to create confusion for our kids when others may do things differently, nor do we want our kids to feel pressured to do something we don't agree with. Staying together during church takes away the awkward pressures that our kids may run into, and ensures that they don't have to deal with those *potential* situations until we believe they are old enough to handle them appropriately.

Furthermore, we want church to be a time for worshipping Jesus, not focused on hanging out with friends. Yes, we want our children to have friends (we've already covered that, haven't we...?), and yes, we want our children to make friends at church, and enjoy fellowshipping with those friends while we are there. But we want to make sure that, especially on Sunday mornings, worshipping Jesus is our family's priority, and we believe worshipping together as a family helps to teach our children that.

Another reason we choose to worship together as a family is that it will allow us to monitor and approve of exactly what material each person in our family is being exposed to. Now again, let me clarify here. That doesn't mean that the children's teachers in our church (or any specific church) are not trustworthy teachers, nor does it mean that the youth leaders are not teaching from the Bible. We feel very blessed to be a part of a congregation who takes *very* seriously the Word of God *in entirety*! We are also extremely thankful that so many people at our church have been gifted with the spiritual gift of teaching, and we are very supportive of them volunteering as they feel led.

In the unlikely event that we *are* exposed to something contradictory from Biblical teaching, though, worshipping together as a family allows us to model a proper reaction for our children. Perhaps we hear something in the message that we discern to be Biblically inconsistent - we can address it during our family discussion afterwards, making sure that our children understand the error. Or perhaps the message presented is so blatantly misleading that we discern it best to remove our family from the support of that teaching altogether, and so get up and leave (again, highly unlikely in our church - this is simply a hypothetical). Or maybe family worship just allows our children to learn what we deem as acceptable worship to Jesus and what we don't - for instance, when we refuse to recognize others or discourage personal recognition during a church service (clapping, standing, etc) because we believe that *Jesus* is the only One deserving of recognition, and not *us*.

By being with us all the time, our children can learn first hand what we discern as appropriate worship, and how to handle what we do not.

Please let me reiterate here that this is *not* a slam against anyone or any department in our church, or in any specific church. We believe that each leader and each department is useful and necessary in spreading the love of Jesus to others, and we are incredibly happy with, and supportive of, each one. We just believe that for our family, it's best that we are all together, learning the same thing.

While these reasons are very important to us, however; our decision to worship together is not necessarily absolute. This decision for our family doesn't mean that we think splitting up is *always* bad, or that we will *never* do it. Again, this is something we will let the Holy Spirit direct us on, rather than make a blanket absolute statement.

In fact, we believe that splitting up sometimes can definitely have benefits - especially when children are very young! Refusing to leave my 3 month old in the nursery for sake of keeping my family together for worship is just silly, and is negating the point. Rest assured, as soon as this mama has felt comfortable, my little Hedges babies have headed straight to our beloved Ms. Peggy and Ms. Betty in the nursery! Having that hour or two every Sunday morning to recharge my batteries and fill up on Jesus for the week is absolutely necessary for my sanity, and that little break for me totally benefits my kids. I have found, through trial and error, that I am a better role model to them throughout the week having had that time to repent, recharge, and refocus.

With that said - I'd like to stop here and just show my appreciation to anyone who volunteers in childcare, for these specific reasons. It's especially a big deal for me (as a stay at home mama, who arguably never gets a break from her kids), as it is often hard for me to leave my tiny little persons in the care of someone else. That's why we are so fortunate that our church is *especially* blessed with nursery volunteers who love little babies. And if you have your own little bundle of joy, I highly encourage you to find a church with a great nursery program that will allow you to have that often much needed little break to worship Jesus too! Ok - moving on!

Also, while our ultimate goal is of course to worship together as a family, we understand that it's not just babies that need to utilize the nursery. We know *well* that small children, or children with special needs, have a difficult time sitting still and staying quiet for extended periods, and to require their presence in church can be both frustrating to the parents, as well as a distraction to those sitting nearby. That's why we believe it is important for our family to utilize the nursery until each individual child has reached an appropriate age where he can attend the lesson and not be a distraction (with that said, we understand that there are parents who may want even their babies in the service with them, and we happily support their decision to follow God's lead in that area).

We also understand that learning how to be still and sit quietly doesn't just happen on it's own. That's why we work diligently to teach our children how to sit still and stay quiet for extended periods of time. We start training them around 18 months old with what we call 'be still time', where we sit them in a chair with nothing to distract them (no toys, no sippy cup, etc), for thirty seconds at a time. Through correction, encouragement, and praise, they begin to learn how to sit still and be quiet, and gradually, we increase the intervals to one minute, five minutes, ten minutes, etc. Pretty soon, our little ones are able to sit still and quiet for thirty to forty-five minutes at a time - which is roughly the length of a lesson at church. Until they master this though, we are happy to use the church nursery!

We also help prepare our little ones for family worship by including our toddlers in as much of the service as we can before taking them to the nursery. This is dependent on a few different factors (age, personality, time of service, etc.); but we love involving them as much as we can, like taking them to the altar for prayer before the service, keeping them with the family during music time, or sitting with them during a children's sermon. These are all ways to help transition them into full family worship! We are confident that with each child, the Lord will direct us in the timing of when to require their presence during the lesson.

Look, this conviction isn't meant to be some strict rule that we won't ever break. I'm sure that we will find ourselves in five different places next Sunday since I've shared all this now (insert head smack)! Instead, it's just a goal that we have and will strive for so as to honor God!

One final thing to note is that, on *occasion* we may choose not attend our normal church service for worship, though this is rare. However, should we for some reason not approve of the planned service, or should we be out of town, we always still try to worship together as a family through music and a family lesson.

CONCLUSION

Well I guess that about does it. You can breathe a sigh of relief now (I know I am!).

Of course this book doesn't cover every last step to success or conviction that we have for our family, but it does highlight some important truths and decisions.

I just want you to be able to use this glimpse into our lives (on the balance beam, remember) as encouragement in your own life, to sacrifice as God leads and convicts you in different areas.

It is my hope in having shared all of this with you, especially 'Part 2' of this book, that you can see our genuine desire to bear fruit and bring glory to Jesus in *everything* we do, and that we can encourage you to do the same.

I also want to reiterate that my transparency of our convictions is not my bragging about how I think we are better than anyone else. I don't think that *at all*. In fact, on the contrary, I'm humbled that I've been given the opportunity to shed light on areas that other families may not have considered.

I'm also incredibly humbled to think that I might be able to bring my Creator glory through encouraging just *one* reader out there to follow through with her own God-given convictions, and in turn bring success to her marriage and family.

The Bible calls us to be a light to the lost, a city on a hill. I believe that sharing the principles of this book with you along with our personal convictions is one way that I can be that light. And I encourage you to do likewise, and imitate us - not our every action, but our devotion and commitment to Christ. Even Paul had confidence enough in what Jesus was doing in his own life to encourage others to imitate him! Kind of scary, and reassuring at the same time!

And, if the only thing you're convinced of now, after reading this book, is that we really are a bunch of crazies, I'm **OK** with that - I just hope it's clear that we are a bunch of crazies for Jesus!

We don't have all the answers (not even close), our lives are not perfect (**REALLY** not even close!), and "all of our righteous acts are like filthy rags" to God (Isaiah 64:6); but the call of God in my life to share these things with you has been crystal clear, in hopes to help women everywhere find a successful marriage and thriving family, and, most importantly, so that God Almighty might be glorified.

I want to leave you with one final thought on our personal list of convictions. We didn't start our married life out so successfully, or with the list of convictions that you just read. We stumbled and fumbled along the way as God taught us, and I know we will keep tripping up here and there as time goes on, and as God chips away and molds us even more into the image of Jesus.
In fact, I'd venture to say not a one of our convictions was truly important to us at the time we said "I do". But God has chipped away at us, and molded us along the way, through our specific circumstances, our past, and our desire for a better future. It's been a painful process, I won't lie; but I can tell that He's refining us for His glory, and I believe that He can use us to help raise up a generation of successful marriages and families.

So, I guess all the secrets to your success are out!

Submission.
Selflessness.
Following through with your convictions.

116

The world will tell you not to. The world will tell you that you're crazy. The world will definitely tell you that *I* am.
But that's ok.
Your marriage, your family... they're worth it. *You're* worth it.

Did you hear that? You're worth it. Just be careful not to confuse worth with deservedness. We all *deserve* eternal death - Hell - for our sins, but Jesus - in His grace - found worth in each of us, enough to step out of His Heavenly throne and come to Earth as the One and only Son of God, to take what we deserved.

He came to die so that we might live - *and live abundantly.*
Let His sacrifice not be in vain for your life.
I encourage you to believe in Him, in His life... His death... and in the defeat of eternal death for us through His resurrection.

Furthermore, I encourage you to trust His plan for your own successful marriage and family (remember, this is not *my* plan!).
So, with confidence, live out this plan so that you, too, can achieve success! Abundant success!
And then share it with others so that they can too!

Finally, *enjoy* your success! *Enjoy* your marriage! *Enjoy* your family!

So what are you waiting for, girls? Success is yours for the taking.

Man up!

(wink!)

DEDICATION PAGE

This book is dedicated to my dad, who taught me to believe in Everything I do today.

Thanks Dad.

SPECIAL THANKS

Where on Earth do I start? There are so many people to thank, and I don't want to miss anyone!

First and foremost,
To my Savior, my Lord, my Provider, my Healer, my Protector, my Comfort, my Peace... my All: Thank You for choosing *me*. Thank You for the cross, for my salvation, and for my eternal security in Heaven. You have my life as a pathetic offering that will never be able to repay the love, mercy, and grace You have shown me, and continue to show me. Thank You for the many blessings You have given to me; I take them for granted daily. Thank You for the convictions that you have placed in my heart, and for the callings you have given me. I ask that You use this book for Your glory. Please bless **THIS** reader with salvation, and meet the needs of **THIS** reader according to Your will. Thank You for the opportunity You have given me to serve You. I can't wait to see You soon.

To my husband, Josh: Thank you for supporting me in this particular endeavor, and for putting up with me through it (and always!). I could not have done this without you. You affirmed this call from God in my life to write this book, guided me in my presentation of this information, prayed for God's will to be done, and dealt with all my imperfections and impatience along the way, including my sporadic, yet time consuming devotion to this project. You picked up the slack I shouldn't have let fall, as I wrote and edited, and edited some more; and you strategically

121

budgeted and selflessly provided the income that you earned to cover the cost of publishing this book in the right timing, all so that others may be blessed. I am so undeserving, and eternally grateful to call you mine. Thanks for marrying me, babe.

To my children, Jackson, Mary, Abby, & Jordan: Thank you for your sweet willingness to overlook my shortcomings as a mother, for your love toward each other, and for your innocence and ability to keep no record of my wrongs. I fall short as your Mama so often, but God uses each of you daily to remind me *why* He called me to write this book. You are the arrows in my quiver, and to say that I am blessed by that is an understatement. You are more dear to me than you will ever know, and I thank God for giving me each of you for a short while.

To my sister, Jenny: You're my best friend. My voice of reason. My partner in crime. My kick in the pants. My accountability. My shoulder to cry on. My confidant. You get me. You make me laugh. You keep me in check. You're honest and loving and trustworthy and dependable. You live for Jesus and teach others to do the same. You are patient and faithful and intentional. Thank you for bringing these pages to life for me in your own life. And... thank you for always checking my kids' windows and cleaning their ears!

To my sister, Becky: Beck, you are the most selfless, flexible, and adaptable person I know; all qualities that I know were given to you by God. Thank you for being such a wonderful model of these things to your selfish, rigid, and stubborn little sister (and to me too... wink!). Thank you so much for your constant love toward me.

To my nisters, Cristina & Emma: Saying 'thank you' doesn't do justice for what all you two have done for me. Along with my kids, *you two* are the ones I spend my days with. *You two* are the ones who see me *constantly* messing up, the ones who *constantly* overlook my shortcomings, and the ones who have *constantly* taken care of the 'behind the scenes' work, so that I could accomplish my callings from God. You guys were the ones sweeping up cheerios, folding clothes, scrubbing toilets, teaching Kindergarten Science and History, and tons more, as I lesson planned, graded papers, fed babies and changed diapers, and at points along the way when I poured my heart out on paper for this book. Without your help, your servant hearts, and your consideration toward me and toward the Kingdom of God, this book wouldn't have been able to be written. My life would truly be a mess without you two (I mean that quite literally!). You *both* are the epitome of a Godly woman, and I can't wait to see what God has in store for your future. From the bottom of my heart, thank you.

To my nieces, Angela & Sara: God has used your precious lives to show me His great love, and confirm certain callings on my life. I am humbled to be even a small part of your lives, and pray that God would use me however He likes as you grow and mature into beautiful young women. I love you!

To my Aunt Janis: You have taught and encouraged me so much through your skill of writing, your commitment to family, your generosity and thoughtfulness, and in your devotion to Jesus. Thank you for *always* being an open door, for never turning me away (no matter what crazy things I have said or done!), and for specifically supporting me in this calling; and most importantly, thank you for **NEVER** saying no to ketchup!

To my Aunt Jeanie: You are comfort. You are love. You are fun. Sentimental. Thoughtful. Encouraging. Smart. Caring. Your words, often few, are wise. You aren't concerned with the ways of the world, and your contentment is admirable. Thank you for always being just the right mix of whatever it is I need, and for coming up with woperdaughter!

To my in-laws: Neither of you know just how much you mean to me, or just how influential you have been in my life. You are both incredibly selfless and generous, and your marriage is one of the most beautiful examples of love I've ever seen. I am so thankful that God chose me to be your **DIL**. I love you both so much.

To Nanny, Ga & Stu: Oh, how I love you all, and how thankful I am for you. Before I even came along, you were praying for me and for my marriage and family - something I will forever be thankful for. Nanny, I've never met a prayer warrior as devoted as you, and Ga & Stu, you guys take the cake on generosity - I've never met a couple as quick to bless others as you. For all you have ever done for our family, and for the incredible influence you've been to us, thank you. You've modeled so much of what God led me to write here, and I was reminded of you all throughout this entire process. I love you heaps.

To my Mama: The last of my family listed here, but the greatest of examples. Mom, you're my model for what a good Christian wife and mother should look like, and there's not one person on the face of this planet that could disagree. Furthermore, unlike me, you've never once opened your mouth about what that should look like - you've only modeled it in your actions. Time and time again, you remind me of what Jesus looks like. You're not a complainer, you're not a pushover, and you're not afraid of hard work (and the list could go on and on and on). The point is, I love you, and I thank you for the example you have set for me. I only hope that I can be half the Mama you are and have always been.

And my amazing friends...
To Meghan, Kristin, Elizabeth, Rachel, Susan, Amy, Mallory, Amie, Brittany, & Lyssa: You girls are my people. My support. My ear to listen to and shoulder to cry on. You are my best friends. The ones that have put up with me for all these years. The ones who, despite my pharisaical nature, have shown me what Jesus truly looks like. You've been the very definition of grace in my life, forgiving my shortcomings, loving me through my faults, and showing me the faithfulness of true friends. For each of your friendships, I am sincerely grateful and eternally thankful. I love you!

To Claire: To find a friend so easy going, so genuine, so generous, so relatable, and yes, so blunt (haha!) has been SUCH a blessing. You quickly became one of my best friends, and I love how our families are so close. You care about what's important, and you don't care about what's not. I have so enjoyed being friends with a fellow germaphobe who lets me cook frozen meals in her oven on our play dates, and who shares my love of animals! Thank you for your Godly influence and friendship. I love you!

To Sarah: I am truly honored to call you a friend. You have been such a blessing in my life as an encourager, a prayer partner and prayer warrior, the voice of reason and perspective, a trusted mentor, accountability, and the one who challenged me to really hide God's word in my heart. You are the epitome of a Godly wife and mother, and you live out these keys to a successful marriage and family daily. You have taught me so much over the years, for which I am forever grateful. I love you!

To my church family at Wynnbrook Baptist Church: I certainly would not be where I am today without your Godly influence and friendship! *Laura, Mandy, Kasey, Julie, Michelle, Dewanna, Emily, Sharon, Jessica, Miss Peggy, Miss Betty, Ms. Jane, Miss Frances, & Miss Frances* (yes there are two!) - your prayers, your honesty, your love, your generosity, your faithfulness to the Lord have all been such a blessing to me. And while these few specific friends mentioned are ladies that I have grown closer to over the years who have shown me Jesus in so many ways, they simply scratch the surface of the friendships I've been blessed with through our body of Christ at Wynnbrook Baptist Church, and there are many who have blessed me in ways they probably don't even know. For instance, *Ms. Gail,* I have been so blessed by watching you sing to the Lord in the choir. And *Lindsey,* I have been moved by your weekly generosity to provide meals for my family when we needed them. And *Ms. Barbara,* I have been so encouraged by the way you teach the children in Sunday School. And *Lisa,* your guidance to me through homeschooling has been invaluable. Time would surely fail me if I continued, but there are countless more ladies I could list who have constantly pointed me to Jesus. I'm also very thankful for the different ministries in our church that have exposed me to the love of Christ through others. From our Sunday School class and care groups, to our Women's Ministry, to our Foster Love Ministry, to our kitchen volunteers, to the nursery workers, and more - I am blessed beyond measure to call each of you friends! You have been the hands and feet of Jesus to me in so many different ways, and I am truly grateful. As I write this, I am thinking of each of you, and thanking God for placing our family at Wynnbrook.

Furthermore, I am thankful for the blessing of my church family at *Wynnton UMC.* Though we are no longer members at Wynnton, that doesn't change the fact that the people of my home church are just as much family to me now as they were the day I was born. *Ms. Dorothy & Ms. Kaye* - you two are especially like family to me and have been all my life. I am so thankful for the Christian influence you've been in my life, and for the love you've shown me since the day I was born. *Ms. Amelia,* you are still just like family too, and I love how you have always shown others the fruits of the Spirit in your life. *Ms. Joy & Ms. Kay,* you two have shown me and countless others the importance of using the gifts God has given you by teaching children to follow after Him. And again, there are so many others who have influenced my life at Wynnton that I could never list them all. I am also especially thankful for a childhood of memories: singing old hymns out of a hymnal, sitting in a pew with my grandparents, and enjoying covered dish luncheons with the whole church congregation, among many other things. I can still close my eyes and see just where each family sat in the sanctuary. The memories here run deep, and the people of Wynnton are forever my family! I wouldn't be who I am today without your love and grace either, and for that I am so thankful.

And an extra special anonymous thanks to two of my friends - you know who you are:
As sincerely as I can possibly say this, thank you for your example. You have excelled in all areas of being a wife, despite the different struggles you faced, and you have shown the world that 'for better or for worse' doesn't mean that you leave when you're unhappy. You've stuck it out through the unimaginable - through adultery, abandonment, conflicts of interest, and more. You've applied the principles of this book, not at my suggestion, but at the direction of the Lord; and you have committed to Him to shine a light to your family and friends through your actions - specifically in your commitment to your marriage vows. You've taught me that the steps and suggestions in this book are not just hard, they are *really* hard; but they are all worth taking. I've learned so much from your unwavering devotion to Jesus; and while your journeys have not been easy, and are still not easy, I've been reminded from your lives that God is a God of miracles, including those of restoration and peace! And because of your willingness to submit, because of your unbelievable selflessness, because of your incredible strength to follow through with *all* of the convictions that God placed on your heart for His glory, I can write this book to encourage others to fight for their families, with *complete* confidence in God's sovereignty. You have been so inspirational with your model of commitment, first to God, and secondly, to your family; and you have absolutely *no* idea the impact you've had on my life, and in my writing this book. I've recalled the stories that you graciously shared with me, the times you let me walk

through heartache with you, and the devotion you've had to Jesus, as I've edited this book so as to encourage others to mimic *you*, with a hopeful outcome. Thank you for teaching me and for allowing me to witness you model all the principles in this book *as* I wrote, without even being aware of what I was writing. You are truly inspirational, and I am incredibly blessed to call you both friend.

Printed in the United States
By Bookmasters